FOUR
BLOOD
M●ONS

JOHN
HAGEE

WORTHY
PUBLISHING

Published by Worthy Publishing, a division of Worthy Media, Inc., 134 Franklin Road, Suite 200, Brentwood, Tennessee 37027.

HELPING PEOPLE EXPERIENCE THE HEART OF GOD

eBook edition available wherever digital books are sold

Audio distributed through Brilliance Audio; visit brillianceaudio.com

---

Library of Congress Control Number: 2013945025

Unless otherwise noted, all Scripture quotations are from the New King James Version of the Bible. Copyright © 1979, 1980, 1982 by Thomas Nelson, Inc., publishers. Used by permission.

Scripture quotations marked KJV are from the King James Version of the Bible. Public domain.

Scripture quotations marked NASB are from the New American Standard Bible, copyright © 1960, 1962, 1963, 1968, 1971, 1972, 1973, 1975, 1977, 1995 by The Lockman Foundation. Used by permission. (www.Lockman.org)

Scripture quotations marked NIV are from the Holy Bible, *New International Version*, *NIV*. Copyright © 1973, 1978, 1984, 2011 by Biblica, Inc.¨ Used by permission of Zondervan. All rights reserved worldwide.

Scripture quotations marked NIV1984 are from the Holy Bible, *New International Version*, *NIV*. Copyright © 1973, 1978, 1984 by Biblica, Inc.¨ Used by permission of Zondervan. All rights reserved worldwide.

Italics added to Scripture quotations are the author's emphasis.

Every effort has been made to obtain permission for the material quoted on pages 215-19. If any required acknowledgments have been omitted, or any rights overlooked, it is unintentional. Please notify the publishers of any omission, and it will be rectified in future editions.

For foreign and subsidiary rights, contact Riggins International Rights Services, Inc.; rigginsrights.com

Published in association with Ted Squires Agency, Nashville, Tennessee

ISBN: 978-1-61795-214-2 (trade paper)
ISBN: 978-1-61795-294-4 (ministry edition)

Cover Design: Christopher Tobias
Ocean photo © Stocktrek Images; Sky image © Igor Kovalchuk/fotolia.com;
  Moon Photo © knickohr/istockphoto.com
Interior Design and Typesetting: Kimberly Sagmiller, FudgeCreative.com

Printed in the United States of America
17 LBM 14

To you . . . the Readers!

My profound gratitude to the millions of you who have chosen to read my books for more than four decades across America and around the world.

Thank you! Gracias! Danke! Merci! Grazie!

CONTENTS

ACKNOWLEDGMENTS

With grateful appreciation to my wife, Diana;
my executive assistant, Jo-Ann; my typist, Melissa;
editor Barbara Dycus; and the fabulous staff
of Worthy Publishing.

SECTION 1

THE SIGNS IN THE HEAVENS

CHAPTER 1
Signs in the Heavens

There will be signs in the sun, in the moon, and in
the stars. . . . Then they will see the Son of Man
coming in a cloud with power and great glory. Now
when these things begin to happen, look up and lift
up your heads, because your redemption draws near.

—LUKE 21:25, 27–28

As the jet plane gracefully circled over the majestic beauty
of Puget Sound, I looked out of the window at the tall and
perfectly shaped spruce trees that surrounded a series of glis-
tening lakes. Along the shoreline stood elegant homes with
boat ramps and fishing docks extending from beautifully

manicured lawns. It was the American paradise that is the gorgeous state of Washington.

The wheels of the jet touched down on the runway with their familiar screech, which is always music to my ears. Every safe landing is a great landing!

The jet rolled to a stop. I unbuckled my seat belt, climbed down the steps, and was refreshingly jolted by the cool breeze on my face. I knew then we were far from the sweltering Texas heat! I began to focus on the reason I was here and what I was to say to the thousands that were gathering for the statewide Night to Honor Israel rally that evening.

Six years earlier, on February 6, 2006, I had invited four hundred of America's foremost evangelical leaders to join me at Cornerstone Church in San Antonio, Texas, to form a national organization called Christians United for Israel. The purpose of our organization is to bring Christians and Jews together in an atmosphere of mutual respect and brotherly love, in order to emphasize that what we have in common is far greater than the differences we have allowed to separate us over the centuries.

If you are not currently a member of Christians United for Israel and desire to stand with Israel and the Jewish people, I strongly encourage you to join us today by going to CUFI.org.

King David said, "You will arise and have compassion on Zion, for it is time to show favor to her; the appointed time has come" (Psalm 102:13 NIV). . . . The appointed time is *now!*

Why Should We Support Israel?

If we are to correctly understand heavenly signs and wonders, it's imperative we grasp the full scope of Scripture and history. The following are five biblical reasons why Christians should be grateful to, and show support for, the nation of Israel and the Jewish people:

1. God Promises to Bless Those Who Bless Israel

"I will bless those who bless you, and I will curse him who curses you" (Genesis 12:3). This is God's pledge to Abraham and the Jewish people for all generations to come. God has promised to bless nations, churches, and individuals who do practical acts of kindness to bless Israel and the Jewish people.

Biblical evidence of God's promised blessing is found in Luke 7, where a Roman centurion who had a sick servant wanted the Rabbi from Nazareth to come into his home and heal his servant. Jesus was an observant Jew; yet He would have to break the laws of Moses to enter the house of a Gentile, who was considered unclean.

The centurion—commander of eighty soldiers—sent the Jewish elders to intercept Jesus. The elders begged Jesus earnestly, saying that the Roman centurion request was deserving of Jesus' healing, "for he loves our nation, and has built us a synagogue" (Luke 7:5).

Jesus healed the sick servant because a Gentile had

performed a practical act of kindness to bless Israel and the Jewish people.

The Bible further supports God's blessing on those who bless Israel with the evidence of Cornelius. Why were Cornelius and his household the first Gentiles to hear the gospel and to receive the outpouring of the Holy Spirit? The answer is found in Acts 10:22, which describes Cornelius the centurion as "a just man, one who fears God and has a good reputation among all the nation of the Jews."

God performed a miracle to motivate the apostle Peter to go to the house of this unclean Gentile. Peter had a vision of a sheet (a prayer shawl) filled with unclean animals (Gentiles), and God commanded him not to call unclean what God had pronounced as clean (Acts 10:9–16). Peter obeyed the message of the vision and went, against religious tradition, to the house of a Gentile to present the gospel.

When Peter shared the gospel with the household of Cornelius, they all received salvation and were filled with the Holy Spirit, and then Peter commanded them to be baptized in water (Acts 10:44–48).

The Holy Spirit was poured out on Cornelius and his household because a Gentile did practical acts of kindness to bless the Jewish people, and true to His promise, God blessed him beyond measure.

I can testify personally that there is no human explanation for the unprecedented blessing of God on Cornerstone

Church and John Hagee Ministries other than the fact that more than thirty years ago we decided to show practical acts of kindness for Israel and the Jewish people. Since that time, God has opened the windows of heaven and blessed us beyond measure.

God's promise is a fact: "I will bless those who bless you."

2. WE ARE COMMANDED TO PRAY FOR THE PEACE OF JERUSALEM

Praying for the peace of Jerusalem is not a request—it's a command! "Pray for the peace of Jerusalem: may they prosper who love you" (Psalm 122:6).

From God's perspective, Jerusalem is the center of the universe. Jerusalem is the city David conquered from the Jebusites three thousand years ago, and it became the capital of Israel forever. May it always be the eternal and undivided capital of Israel, and may peace be within her walls and prosperity within her palaces (Psalm 122:7).

Jerusalem is where Abraham offered Isaac on Mount Moriah. Jerusalem is where Jeremiah and Isaiah penned principles of righteousness that became the moral compass for Western civilization. And outside of its gates Jesus Christ, the Son of David, was crucified for the sins of the world.

According to biblical prophecy, Jerusalem is the past, present, and future of the world! From this city, Jesus will rule planet earth with a rod of iron, and of His kingdom there shall be no end (Isaiah 9:7; Luke 1:33).

When you pray for Jerusalem, you are praying for world peace. History proves that when there is peace in Jerusalem, there is peace in the world. When there is war in Jerusalem, the blood flows on planet earth. The universe revolves around Jerusalem. I quote my friend Dr. Graham Lacey, "As long as there is Jerusalem there is God; and as long as there is God there is Jerusalem."

3. WE ARE COMMANDED TO BE WATCHMEN ON THE WALLS OF ISRAEL

God commands us through the prophet Isaiah to be watchmen on the walls of Jerusalem (62:6). We are commanded by God, through the prophet Isaiah, to speak up and defend Israel and the Jewish people when they are slandered, attacked by their enemies, and are subjected to any callous act of anti-Semitism. Isaiah writes:

> For Zion's sake I will not hold My peace,
> And for Jerusalem's sake I will not rest. . . .
> I have set watchmen on your walls, O Jerusalem;
> They shall never hold their peace day or night.
> You who make mention of the LORD, do not keep silent.
>
> (62:1, 6)

4. WE ARE COMMANDED TO MINISTER TO ISRAEL IN MATERIAL THINGS

Another biblical reason we support Israel is given by the apostle Paul: "For if the Gentiles have been partakers of their spiritual things [the Jewish people], their duty [the Gentiles] is also to minister to them [the Jewish people] in material things" (Romans 15:27).

What are the "spiritual things" Paul is referring to?

- The Jewish people have given to us the written Word of God.
- The Jewish people have given to us the patriarchs: Abraham, Isaac, and Jacob.
- The Jewish people have given to us the Old Testament prophets: Ezekiel, Isaiah, Jeremiah, Daniel, Hosea, Joel, Amos, Obadiah, Jonah, Micah, Nahum, Habakkuk, Zephaniah, Haggai, Zechariah, and Malachi.
- The Jewish people have given to us the first family of Christianity: Mary, Joseph, and Jesus. Take Jesus out of Christianity and there is no Christianity.
- The Jewish people have given to us the twelve disciples and the apostle Paul.

Consider the monumental contribution given to us by the seed of Abraham. For this reason Jesus said in John 4:22, "For salvation is of the Jews."

If you take away the Jewish contribution to Christianity, there would be no Christianity. Judaism does not need Christianity to explain its existence; Christianity, however, cannot explain its existence without Judaism.

When I refer to Christianity I am referencing the teachings of Christ, which were based on the principles of Judaism—not the deeds of polluted historic Christianity.

Historic Christianity has left an evil legacy. It is responsible for the Crusades, in which Jewish people from Europe to Jerusalem were slaughtered in seven major pogroms (crusades). The first crusade was declared by Pope Urban II in 1095. The Crusaders were rapists and thieves, forgiven in advance by the reigning pope for any sins they might commit while on their holy campaign to liberate Jerusalem from the "infidels."

Not one Christian in a hundred today can answer the question: "How is it that Christianity, born through the teachings of a Jewish rabbi named Jesus of Nazareth, could three hundred years later kill Jews in the name of God?"

There is a dramatic difference between historic Christianity and the teachings of Jesus Christ. I publicly state that I am not a follower of historic Christianity; I am a follower of Jesus Christ!

5. JESUS ENTREATED THE CHURCH TO SUPPORT ISRAEL

We should support Israel and the Jewish people because it was Jesus' final request to His church. Jesus said in Matthew 25:40:

Assuredly, I say to you, inasmuch as you did it to one
of the least of these *My brethren* [the Jewish people],
you did it to Me.

Jesus never called the Gentiles *His brethren* until after the
cross. Before the cross we were, as described by the apostle
Paul, outside the covenants of Israel, without God and without hope, of all men most miserable (Ephesians 2:12; 1 Corinthians 15:19).

Gentile Christians can look at the day of the cross and
shout for joy. It was there we were grafted into the original
olive tree (Romans 11:17). It was there our sins were forgiven,
buried in the deepest sea, never to be remembered anymore
(Jeremiah 31:34). It was there that our sicknesses and diseas-
es were removed and we received divine health, for "by His
stripes we are healed" (Isaiah 53:5).

It was at the cross that Jesus took our poverty and gave to
us the riches of Abraham. We who were "not a people" (1 Peter 2:10) were adopted and became "kings and priests to His
God" (Revelation 1:6), "ambassadors for Christ" (2 Corinthians 5:20), and have been taken from rags to royalty through
the precious blood of the virgin-born, "the only begotten Son
of God" (John 3:18). The curse of death, hell, and the grave was
broken, and we were given eternal life; hallelujah for the cross!

God's Gentile assignment toward the Jewish people is to
show them what they have not seen from historic Christianity

in two thousand years—*the pure and unconditional love of God*!

> Let your light so shine before men, that they may see your good works [practical acts of kindness] and glorify your Father in heaven.
>
> (MATTHEW 5:16)

Jesus said, "I was hungry and you gave Me food; I was thirsty and you gave Me drink; I was a stranger and you took Me in; I was naked and you clothed Me; I was sick and you visited Me; I was in prison and you came to Me" (Matthew 25:35–36).

Jesus makes it very clear that it's not what you feel about the Jewish people that is the acid test, for Jesus didn't say, "I was hungry and you *felt sorry for* Me; I was thirsty and you *felt concern for* Me; I was a stranger and you *felt pity for* Me." I often hear pastors, evangelists, and Christians say, "I really like Israel" or "I like the Jewish people." Jesus couldn't care less what you like or don't like; He's looking for action. What will you do? What practical acts of kindness have you or your church done to demonstrate your love for Israel as mentioned in Matthew 25:40? What *action* have you taken to support Israel?

Stop talking about what you *feel* . . . and start taking *action* by showing practical acts of kindness toward God's chosen people. Simply put, "Don't tell me you love me. Show me!"

CHRISTIANS UNITED FOR ISRAEL

When I stood before those four hundred evangelical leaders at Cornerstone Church on February 6, 2006, asking them to join me in a historic effort to lovingly and unconditionally support Israel and the Jewish people, I fully expected a theological argument that would have made the battle of the Alamo look like a backyard Texas tea party.

But the free-for-all didn't happen! Instead, the most influential spiritual leaders in the nation mutually agreed to stand up and speak up for Zion's sake. No debates. No axes to grind. No pontification on, "One thing we must make clear about our differences is . . . blah, blah, blah." Nothing but a divine moment of unconditional unity.

With one voice, we declared that Israel had the right to exist, the right to secure defensible borders, and the right to defend themselves by themselves against any enemy. The blessings that God promised in Psalm 133 has become a reality; as this book goes to print, Christians United for Israel has more than 1.3 million members in America, with nations around the world asking to become a part of this voice of Jewish-Christian unity.

How good and pleasant it is when brothers live together in unity! It is like precious oil poured on the head, running down on the beard, running down on Aaron's beard, down upon the collar of his robes. It

is as if the dew of Hermon were falling on Mount
Zion. For there the LORD bestows his blessing, even
life forevermore.

(PSALM 133 NIV1984)

One of the blessings Christians United for Israel has af-
forded me is the many new friendships with a vast number of
pastors who have come together under one banner in support
of Israel. As one pastor stated, "Pastor Hagee, this is more than
Christians United for Israel; this is Israel uniting Christians!"

ON THE ROAD TO EL SHADDAI

Six years after CUFI was born Diana and I got in the waiting
black Suburban for the short trip to the church pastored by
Mark Biltz of El Shaddai Ministries, where the Night to Honor
Israel would be conducted. Spiritual leaders from across the
city and state would attend our first event in the state of Washington. The air was charged with excitement and expectation.

As we drove to the church, I could not get over the breathtaking beauty of Puyallup, Washington, and how cool it was in
the summer. In Texas, the month of August is so unbearably
hot that lizards climb on steam pipes trying to cool off in the
one-hundred-plus-degree temperature.

We arrived at the church where Pastor Mark Biltz and his
gracious staff met us at the front doors. It was my first time to
meet Pastor Biltz, and it's a moment I shall never forget.

Within minutes we were discussing the seven feasts of Israel and their connections to the Lord's first and second coming. I recognized that Pastor Biltz was a Bible scholar par excellence who understood the Jewish roots of Christianity like few people I've ever met.

During our conversation, he asked me if I had ever studied the sun, moon, and stars as a source of prophetic revelation. My answer was quick and truthful.

"No."

Pastor Biltz immediately responded, "You should! I believe God is trying to speak to us, and we're not listening!"

We walked into the church, and I didn't give our conversation about the sun, moon, and stars a second thought. I was more concerned about speaking to the thousands of people waiting in the church's auditorium.

That night, as I walked onstage with Pastor Biltz and Rabbi Daniel Lapin, one of America's celebrated Torah scholars, to celebrate the Night to Honor Israel, I listened to the sound of the shofar, blown with power and clarity. The long blast . . . the short blast . . . the sweet, thunderous sound reverberated through the auditorium, bringing tears to my eyes—and I am not the weepy type.

As I listened to the divine sound echoing through the packed building, I was reminded of the words of the apostle Paul:

Behold, I tell you a mystery: We shall not all sleep, but

we shall all be changed—in a moment, in the twinkling of an eye, at the last trumpet [shofar]. For the trumpet [shofar] will sound, and the dead will be raised.

(1 CORINTHIANS 15:51–52)

Following the beautiful music of the evening, Rabbi Lapin gave an inspiring speech. He was followed by Pastor Biltz, whose scriptural knowledge concerning the seven feasts and their message to the church today was simply off the charts. Then I presented the biblical reasons for supporting Israel. The wonderful evening came to a joyous conclusion without protestors, security concerns, or a single audio blemish. It was, by every standard of measurement, a magnificent night!

The next morning our entourage climbed aboard the plane bound for the land of the blazing sun—San Antonio, Texas. I had been in four states in three days where I made four speeches, stood for hundreds of photos, and signed enough books to break the back axles in a two-ton truck; we were all fighting jetlag and fatigue.

The plane took off with a roar of the engine, and within minutes Diana was sleeping like she was stretched out on a Posturepedic mattress. I have a confession to make: in the best of situations I have a hard time sleeping . . . period.

For me to sleep six hours, my maximum, I need a room that's absolutely dark, totally quiet, and completely still. Bouncing through the air on an airplane in turbulence at a speed of five hundred miles per hour is like riding a wild Brahman bull at the National Championship Rodeo in Las Vegas.

I glanced at Diana in deep sleep and felt the spirit of resentment creeping in. If deep and prolonged sleep is a guarantee of long life, Diana will live to be one hundred twenty years old . . . *minimum!*

As we climbed to forty thousand feet, and the pilots searched for clear air at an altitude high enough to escape the turbulence, I cinched my seat belt tighter and thought of Jesus' words to His disciples: He said, "Lo, I am with you always" (Matthew 28:20).

In the midst of the storm, my mind went back to Pastor Mark's question: "Have you ever considered the sun, moon, and stars in the study of prophecy?" Having studied the Bible for fifty-four years and authored numerous books on the subject of prophecy, my mind is a database of prophetic Scripture. Genesis 1:14 came to my mind, which declares that God created the sun, moon, and stars (signals) in the heavens.

ASTRONOMY VERSUS ASTROLOGY

Since we will be discussing the sun, moon, and stars as they relate to the Bible and the people of Israel, I want to avoid any possible confusion by clarifying the difference between astronomy and astrology.

Astronomy is the science of studying the movements and positions of planets and stars. For example, the North Star never moves. Knowing where the North Star is has helped captains of ships sail the seven seas of earth for centuries. God Almighty created the stars, and He "calls them all by name" (Psalm 147:4).

Astrology is the worship of stars, which is occultic and pagan. People who make choices based on the stars are seeking guidance for their lives from things created rather than from the Creator. This is a violation of the law of Almighty God (Romans 1:20–21; Exodus 20:4).

In this book, our discussion of the stars and moon in biblical prophecy is based on the Word of God, history, and the science of astronomy—and *never* refers to astrology.

GOD'S HIGH-DEFINITION BILLBOARD

As I thought about the sun, moon, and stars as sources of prophetic direction, I considered the words of Joel 2:30–31:

> I will show wonders in the heavens and in the earth:
> Blood and fire and pillars of smoke.
> The sun shall be turned into darkness,
> And the moon into blood,
> *Before the coming* of the great and awesome day of the LORD.

I remembered that the apostle Peter, on the day of Pentecost, made nearly the exact same remarks, as recorded in Acts 2:19–20:

I will show wonders in heaven above
And signs in the earth beneath:
Blood and fire and vapor of smoke.
The sun shall be turned into darkness,
And the moon into blood,
Before the coming of the great and awesome day of the LORD.

What does "moon into blood" refer to in these two verses? I learned later in my research that this astronomical event is actually called a Blood Moon. A Blood Moon occurs during a total lunar eclipse; the moon does not actually turn to blood, but it does appear blood-red.

If we are going to see these wonders in the heavens *before* the coming of the Lord, how long before His coming will we see them? The Bible gives no answer other than the words of Jesus to His disciples:

Of that day and hour no one knows, not even the angels of heaven, but My Father only.

(MATTHEW 24:36)

Jesus said, "There will be signs in the sun, in the moon, and in the stars. . . . When these things begin to happen, look up and lift up your heads, because your redemption draws near" (Luke 21:25, 28).

In the prophetic words Jesus spoke to His disciples on the

Mount of Olives, He stated:

> Immediately after the tribulation of those days the sun
> will be darkened [solar eclipse], and the moon will
> not give its light [lunar eclipse]; the stars will fall from
> heaven, and the powers of the heavens will be shaken
> [nuclear warfare?]. Then [after the signs in the heav-
> ens] the Son of Man will appear in heaven.
>
> (MATTHEW 24:29–30)

What do all these prophecies have in common? They all involve specific signs in the heavens preceding coming global events! Does God use the sun, moon, and stars to communicate with us? Does He use the heavens as His own personal, high-definition billboard to announce things to come?

The answer is *yes*, according to Genesis 1:14, which states:

> Then God said, "Let there be lights in the firmament
> of the heavens to divide the day from the night; and let
> them be for *signs* and seasons."

The Hebrew word for "sign" is *owth*, which also translates as "signals." Therefore, based on the Bible, God uses the sun, moon, and stars as *signals* to mankind. He uses the heavens as His divine billboard announcing coming events.

What is God trying to say to us?

SIGNS OVER RUSSIA

In late February 2013, the world was astounded when a blazing meteor exploded over Russia. NASA (The National Aeronautics and Space Administration) reported that the fifty-five-foot-wide rock, which weighed an estimated ten thousand tons, entered the earth's atmosphere traveling forty-four thousand miles per hour.

NASA estimated that the energy released as the meteors disintegrated in the atmosphere was 500 kilotons, around 30 times the size of the nuclear bomb dropped on Hiroshima in 1945.[1]

The ten-thousand-ton meteor lit up the Russian skies before crashing into the earth, causing shockwaves that injured twelve hundred people and damaged thousands of homes in an event unprecedented in modern times.

A priest near the explosion site called it "an act of God."[2] A fireball traveling at forty-four thousand miles per hour with a long, blazing white tail visible one hundred twenty-five miles away has to be considered a *sign from heaven*.

John the Revelator pulls back the curtain of the future and clearly reveals that God will use signs in the heavens during the Great Tribulation to communicate His wrath and judgment to the world. John writes:

Then the second angel sounded [the trumpet]: And something like a great mountain burning with fire was thrown into the sea. . . . Then the third angel sounded [the trumpet]: And a great star fell from heaven, burning like a torch, and it fell on a third of the rivers and on the springs of water. The name of the star is Wormwood. A third of the waters became wormwood, and many men died from the water, because it was made bitter.

(REVELATION 8:8, 10–11)

God is going to shake the world with "signs in the heavens" when He personally destroys the Iranian and Russian armies that invade Israel in the Gog-Magog War of Ezekiel 38. This won't be the first time; God Himself stoned the five armies that attacked Israel in Joshua 10:

And it happened, as they [the five armies] fled before Israel . . . that the LORD cast down large hailstones from heaven . . . and they died. There were more who died from the hailstones than the children of Israel killed with the sword. (v. 11)

The meteor that crashed into Russia—the nation that swore there was no God—was sent a supernatural FedEx message that basically said: I am God, and there is none like

Me, not in the heavens above nor the world beneath. From everlasting to everlasting I am God. (This truth is based on Isaiah 46:9 and Psalm 41:13.)

The fact that God hurled stones from the heavens to defend Israel in Joshua 10 is living proof that God will use stones as a weapon of war to crush the invading Iranian and Russian forces coming against Israel. This will happen as recorded by the prophet Ezekiel in chapter 38:

> And I will bring him to judgment with pestilence and bloodshed; I will rain down on him, on his troops, and on the many peoples who are with him . . . great hailstones, fire, and brimstone. . . . Then they shall know that I am the LORD. (vv. 22–23)

Signs in the heavens are coming to the enemies of Israel!

SIGNS IN THE SUN

In recent dissertations scientists analyzed the uncommon signs of giant solar eruptions.

Tariq Malik, managing editor of Space.com, reports:

> The sun unleashed a monster eruption of super-hot plasma Friday [November 16, 2012] in back-to-back solar storms captured on camera by a NASA spacecraft. The giant eruption, called a solar prominence,

occurred at 1:00 A.M. EST (0600 GMT), with another event flaring up four hours later.[3]

In an interview with George Norry on Coast to Coast radio, physicist Michio Kaku stated that he is becoming very concerned about the recent solar flares, indicating that "the sun is having a temper tantrum, and it's getting worse and worse." He continued by saying, "My greatest fear is the earth getting hit by a large solar flare, and all hell could break loose!"[4]

In an earlier video lecture, Professor Kaku indicated, "We are sitting ducks for solar flares." If a catastrophic solar flare "were to happen today . . . it would wipe out most of our satellites . . . black out our weather satellites, GPS systems, telecommunications, the Internet. Power stations would be vulnerable, not just in one city . . . but in cities simultaneously across the entire planet earth. Refrigeration would be knocked out for perhaps weeks at a time. . . . Society as we know it would be thrown back perhaps a hundred years into the past."[5]

Professor Kaku confirms that the world is watching signs in the sun, which are going to increase in frequency and will eventually hit the earth—it's just a matter of time.

THE CHALLENGE

Diana arose from her deep and untroubled sleep as the wheels of the jet touched down on the runway. My mind raced with the anticipation of finding the answers to Pastor Mark's challenging question: "Have you ever considered the sun, moon, and stars in the study of prophecy?" I asked myself, "Was God using the signs in the heavens to show us the world tomorrow?"

I disembarked from the plane to be met by the heat of the blazing Texas sun, thinking, *A total solar eclipse might be a good thing right about now!*

I was on my way home to begin a search of the sun, moon, and stars and how they relate to Israel in the past, present, and future. I thought of what King David declared in the Psalms:

The heavens declare the glory of God;
  the skies proclaim the work of his hands.
Day after day they pour forth speech;
  night after night they reveal *knowledge.*
They have *no speech,* they use *no words*;
  no sound is heard from them.
Yet their *voice* goes out into all the earth,
  their *words* to the ends of the world.

(19:1–4)

The history of the world is about to change forever, and God is sending us messages on His high-definition billboard by speaking to us in the heavens—using the Four Blood Moons; the question is . . . are we listening?

CHAPTER 2
The Star in the East

We have seen His star in the East
and have come to worship him.

—MATTHEW 2:2

I always enjoy coming home!

In years past I was greeted by the cheering mob of my five children, who were always glad to see Dad. Now they are all married, and God has blessed us with thirteen of the most beautiful grandchildren on the face of the earth. We are very fortunate to have all five children and their families live in town, so when we return from a trip several of the grandchildren will come by to hug Nana and Papa. I *do* love coming home! I threw my bags onto the bed, took a quick shower to wake up, and made a fresh pot of hot coffee to stimulate my tired mind and stiff body.

As the coffee brewed, I sat at the desk in my office, which had been masterfully designed by Diana. She converted an exercise room that I didn't use enough into an office that I now use too much! I like to read much more than I like to run on a treadmill. I have more than five thousand books in my personal library, with all contents coded so I can resource an ocean of information with a click of a computer key; my journey was about to begin!

I sat behind my desk and reached for a legal tablet to organize the swarm of thoughts buzzing through my brain into logical and scriptural order. All fresh revelation from God must be biblically sound—rock solid! If the basic premise in any new concept has the smallest amount of leaven, the final conclusion will be *puffed up* and filled with hot air. All who preach or teach the Bible have a mandate from Paul to "Preach the word!" (2 Timothy 4:2).

I began my study of the signs in the heavens with one of the most controversial verses in the Bible: "In the beginning God created the heavens and the earth" (Genesis 1:1).

In the Beginning . . .

"In the beginning" could have taken place millions of years ago in man's way of measuring time. If your child is taught that scientists have found carbon-dated rocks millions of years old, this finding in no way counters God's creation timeline.

God's time clock, which is measured by the Seven Ages and Dispensations, does not start ticking until Genesis 1:3. The Scriptures divide the period from the creation of Adam to the "new heaven and a new earth" of Revelation 21:1 into seven unequal periods, called dispensations (Ephesians 3:2), or ages (Ephesians 2:7).

These periods are marked off in Scripture by God's method of dealing with mankind. The Seven Ages and Dispensation are: Innocence, Conscience, Human Government, Promise, Law, Grace, and the Millennial Reign of Christ.

"Created" in Hebrew is *bara*, which means "to make from nothing."[1] God did not come to an established earth and rearrange what was here; He made something beautifully magnificent and awesomely wondrous out of *nothing*!

"God created the heavens . . ." The word *heavens* is plural because there are three heavens in Scripture. There is the first heaven, which we see with our naked eye, consisting of the sun, moon, and stars.

The second heaven is where Satan has his throne. God converses with Satan in the second heaven (Job 1:6–8) and casts him out in the book of Revelation (20:1–3).

The apostle Paul was given a guided tour through the eternal heaven, which he refers to as the "third heaven"

(2 Corinthians 12:2). Paul, who could say more in less time than any author in recorded history, after seeing the grandeur of heaven simply recorded the following description for future generations:

> Eye has not seen, nor ear heard,
> Nor have entered into the heart of man
> The things which God has prepared for those who love
> Him.
>
> (1 Corinthians 2:9)

You often hear people speaking of the seventh heaven; it doesn't exist unless you are on an ethereal drug-induced trip!

Why is Genesis 1:1 controversial? Why does the prince of darkness hate this verse and every concept of this verse? Because if you don't believe Genesis 1:1 and trust the Holy Spirit when He tells you of the creation, why would you trust Him when He tells you about the Father's plan of salvation for your eternal soul in John 3:16?

If you don't believe Genesis 1:1, you have no solid foundation to believe the rest of Scripture. You can't believe that God parted the Red Sea for Moses or stopped the sun for Joshua and you can't possibly believe that God controls the sun, moon, and stars and creates signs to appear in the heavens at specific times in history.

If what God's Word says about the creation is not true, why would you believe His Word when He says, "Call to Me, and I will answer you, and show you great and mighty things, which you do not know" (Jeremiah 33:3)? If Genesis 1:1 is not true, why bother believing the remainder of the Word of God?

GOD'S CONTROL OVER THE HEAVENS

I asked myself the question as I continued my research, *What is the Bible's evidence that God totally controls the sun, moon, and stars?*

I read the story of Joshua and the children of Israel, who were attacked by the armies of five kings seeking to annihilate God's chosen (Joshua 10:1–13).

> The LORD said to Joshua, "Do not fear them, for I have delivered them into your hand; not a man of them shall stand before you." Joshua therefore came upon them suddenly, having marched all night from Gilgal. So the LORD routed them before Israel, killed them with a great slaughter at Gibeon. . . . And it happened, as they fled before Israel and were on the descent of Beth Horon, that the LORD cast down large hailstones from heaven on them as far as Azekah, and they died. There were more who died from the hailstones than the children of Israel killed with the sword.
>
> (vv. 8–11)

Keep this story in mind for it will come back in living color in the Gog-Magog War, which we will discuss later in this book. The story of Joshua continues. . . .

Then Joshua spoke to the LORD in the day when the LORD delivered up the Amorites before the children of Israel, and he said in the sight of Israel:
"Sun, stand still over Gibeon;
And Moon, in the Valley of Aijaon."
So the sun stood still,
And the moon stopped,
Till the people had revenge
Is this not written in the Book of Jasher? So the sun stood still in the midst of heaven, and did not hasten to go down for about a whole day.

(vv. 12–13)

God, the Creator of heaven and earth, took total control of the sun and the moon, which did not move "for about a whole day" (v. 13). For "about a whole day" would be almost twenty-four hours.

God's complete control of the sun is beyond the mental power of man to grasp. The sun is 109 times larger than planet earth. The sun is 27 million degrees Fahrenheit at the core and 10 million degrees Fahrenheit on the surface.[2]

On August 31 [2012] the sun expelled a cloud of 100,000-degree Fahrenheit plasma at more than 900 miles per second. NASA's newest sun-viewing satellite, the Solar Dynamic Observatory, tracked the vast filament, which measured about 30 earths across.[3]

The awesome God we serve created and totally controls this powerful sun!

Additional biblical evidence of God's complete control of the blazing sun is demonstrated in the story of Hezekiah. The prophet Isaiah visited King Hezekiah and told him he was going to die (2 Kings 20:1). Don't you know that if your pastor, priest, or rabbi came to your house and told you God told him you were going to die, you would want to change churches or synagogues immediately!

When Isaiah gave Hezekiah the bad news, Hezekiah turned his face to the wall and prayed, reminding God of how faithfully he had served the Lord all the days of his life.

God heard Hezekiah's petitions and sent the prophet Isaiah back to Hezekiah to inform him that he would not die; instead, God added fifteen years to his life.

Think of it! The power of prayer changed the mind of God.

That was indeed good news, but it was common in the Jewish faith to ask God for a sign so Hezekiah did exactly that:

Hezekiah said to Isaiah, "What is the sign that the LORD will heal me?" Then Isaiah said, "This is the sign to you from the LORD, that the LORD will do the thing which He has spoken: shall the shadow [of the sun on the sundial] go forward ten degrees or go backward ten degrees?" And Hezekiah answered, "It is an easy thing for the shadow to go down ten degrees [because the sun would be setting, which is normal]; no, but let the shadow go backward ten degrees." So Isaiah the prophet cried out to the LORD, and He brought the shadow ten degrees backward, by which it had gone down on the sundial of Ahaz.

(2 KINGS 20:8–11)

Hezekiah wanted a supernatural sign, not a natural one. When God caused the shadow of the sundial to back up ten degrees, He didn't just stop time—He reversed time. He made the sun and time itself go backward. That's supernatural and absolute control!

I believe that the exact amount of time Joshua required to win the battle against the five armies that attacked Israel in Joshua 10, and the amount of time that the sun went backward as a sign to Hezekiah in 2 Kings 20, balanced the solar clock.

That is power my friends, and that is the kind of God we serve!

WISE MEN FOLLOWED THE STAR

Consider the story of the wise men that followed the star sent from God in search of the new born King (Matthew 2:2). Their declaration that they had come to worship the "King of the Jews" terrified Herod the Great.

Who was Herod the Great? Herod became the ruler of the Holy Land under the Romans around 40 BC. He was called *great* because he was the master architect of projects in Caesarea, Jericho, Masada, as well as the wall around the Old City of Jerusalem, built during the time of the Second Temple, which still stands to this day.

Herod was also a wicked maniac who murdered nine of his ten wives on the mere paranoid suspicion that they may have been unfaithful. Herod *knew* he was hated, so he demanded that his son be executed on the day of his own death so that Israel would have a reason to mourn.

Herod the Great was the demonized despot who ordered the Massacre of the Innocents which was the execution of all male Jewish infants in Bethlehem. He feared that a king born of the Jews would challenge his throne.

Herod's corrupt administration could not endure a tidal wave of messianic fever among the Jewish people; revolts were born in such atmospheres. So when the Magi made their declaration that they had come to worship the King of the Jews, Herod called his chief priest to search for a prophetic record of a child who could possibly fit this description. The chief priest came back to Herod with the writings of the prophet Micah, which read:

> But you, Bethlehem Ephrathah,
> Though you are little among the thousands of Judah,
> Yet out of you shall come forth to Me
> The One to be Ruler in Israel. (5:2)

THE KEY TO THE MAGI'S QUEST

The wise men understood the meaning of Micah's prophecy. Therefore, let us turn the key of Scripture to the story of Jacob, the patriarch, and discover the link between the Tribe of Judah and the "One to be Ruler in Israel."

When Jacob, on his deathbed, was giving the prophetic blessing to his twelve sons, he stretched out his right hand, laid it on Judah's head, and spoke these words:

> Judah is a lion's whelp. . . .
> The scepter shall not depart from Judah,
> Nor a lawgiver from between his feet,
> Until Shiloh comes;
> And to Him shall be the obedience of the people.
> Binding his donkey to the vine,
> And his donkey's colt to the choice vine,
> He washed his garments in wine,
> And his clothes in the blood of grapes. (GENESIS 49:9–11)

This is one of the most significant and profound prophecies in the Bible. Consider the type and shadow of Jacob's words and the revelation of Jesus Christ: "Judah is a lion's whelp" (v. 9) and Jesus Christ is "the Lion of the tribe of Judah" (Revelation 5:5).

What Is a Scepter? (v. 10)

The scepter is the golden rod of authority held by a king as he sits on his throne ruling his kingdom. God, the Father, appointed Christ, His Son, heir of all things and He will ultimately hold the scepter of righteousness (Hebrew 1:1–8).

Who Is Shiloh? (v.10)

Shiloh is the ruler to whom the scepter belongs, and it is also a place of rest referring to "the peaceful One." Christ will be the only Ruler who brings rest and tranquility to Israel and the world. Remember, Jesus said, "Come to Me, all you who labor and are heavy laden, and I will give you rest" (Matthew 11:28).

Jacob is painting a prophetic picture for his son Judah as he describes the Son of God, Jesus Christ, who would change the destiny of mankind forever.

Not only is Jesus Christ from the tribe of Judah . . .

Not only do His nail-pierced hands hold the scepter as the Son of David, Messiah, and King of kings . . .

Not only is Jesus Christ Shiloh . . .

He also fulfilled Micah's foretelling of the donkey by sending His disciples to find tied to the vine the colt that Jesus rode into Jerusalem on Passover (Mark 11:2), just before His crucifixion.

And finally, Christ washed His garments in wine.

In the Bible, wine is a symbol of joy. Jesus changed water into wine at the wedding feast of Cana so that there would be complete joy at the celebration (John 2:1–11). "He washed . . . his clothes in the blood of grapes" (Genesis 49:11). The meaning of this verse is a picture of Christ crushing the enemies of Israel, as one stomps grapes to crush them in the making of new wine.

What Jacob spoke over Judah applies to our Lord Jesus. He is the Ruler of all His Father's children, and the Conqueror of all His Father's enemies. He is the Lion of the tribe of Judah. To Him belongs the scepter for He is the Lawgiver. In Him, there is sufficient abundance to nourish and refresh man's soul, producing supernatural joy.

The prophecy about Jesus does not start in Matthew—*it starts in Genesis* with breathtaking power and accuracy.

The Magi followed the star that would lead them to Jesus, who is the "Star" (Numbers 24:17), "the Root and the Offspring of David, and the Bright Morning Star" (Revelation 22:16).

Do you need direction for your life? Follow the star of Bethlehem; it will lead to Christ. Wise men looked for Him then and wise men still follow Him today (Matthew 2:9).

The abovementioned accounts prove beyond a shadow of a doubt that God has absolute control of the sun, moon, and stars. He has used them in the past to send signals to humanity that something *big* was about to happen. The heavens are still God's billboard that sends signals to us today—but are we watching for them?

SIGNS IN THE SUN, MOON, AND STARS

We have established that God, the Father, spoke through the prophets using the sun, moon, and stars. He then sent His Son on an earthly mission to speak of things yet to come. Did Jesus speak about the signs in the heavens and on the earth? Absolutely!

When the disciples came to Jesus on the Mount of Olives and asked Him, ". . . what will be the sign of Your coming and of the end of the age?" He did not rebuke them but answered them by encouraging them to look for the signs on the earth and in the heavens (Matthew 24).

Jesus told them to beware of deception, which would be followed by wars and rumors of wars, famines, pestilence, earthquakes, the attack on Jerusalem by the Romans, and "great tribulation, such as has not been since the beginning of the world until this time [could this be the Holocaust?]" (v. 21). He said that "unless those days were shortened, no flesh would be saved; but for the elect's sake [the Jewish people] those days will be shortened" (v. 22).

Jesus continued in Matthew 24:33: "When you see all these things [these physical signs], know that it [your redemption, according to Luke 21:28] is near—at the doors!"

Jesus ended His teaching session with His disciples by warning all generations not to attempt to set an exact date in which He would return (Matthew 24:36).

Although, Jesus warned us about setting a specific day, He did tell us to watch for signs of His coming. He not only gave His twelve disciples the prophecy in Matthew 24, but also He told them, "there will be signs in the sun, in the moon, and in the stars" (Luke 21:25).

EUREKA!

Though I had applied the study of the stars relative to the creation and the birth of Christ, I had yet to discover the connection that Pastor Mark had asked me to make: how were the sun, moon, and stars linked to the study of prophecy?

I searched the Scriptures for a new revelation with that specific question in mind and came to two verses that shouted out to me!

The sun will be turned to darkness and the moon to blood before the coming of the great and dreadful day of the LORD.

(JOEL 2:31 NIV)

The sun will be turned to darkness and the moon to blood before the coming of the great and glorious day of the Lord.

(ACTS 2:20)

What did these two verses have in common? It was the blood moons! Now my blood pressure was up and my mind was racing with questions!

I knew they related to prophecy, but what were they saying? What was a blood moon? Have they appeared before? Were they coming again? I turned on my computer and started searching for scientific evidence supporting the blood moons. I must confess I am no computer whiz so I found my expedition most exasperating!

After more than an hour of finding nothing, I was ready to quit when it occurred to me that maybe God was using the heavens to send a sign to Israel and the Jewish people. I began a more focused search; I went to the NASA site and suddenly, *there it was*! It leaped off the screen, and I gasped with excitement.

The sun, moon, and stars *are unmistakably connected to Israel and biblical prophecy*—and *that* connection inspired this book. God will use them to light up the heavens with an *urgent, top-priority message* for all mankind.

What is God saying to us?

How does the past hold the secret to the future?

What is about to happen on planet earth?

Everything is about to change . . . forever!

Keep reading, because this message from God is so urgent to *Him* that He sovereignly arranged the sun and the moon to perfectly align themselves to create a *Tetrad*—four consecutive blood moons. He didn't do this just one time—but Tetrads linked to Jewish history have happened only three times in more than five hundred years. *And it's about to happen for a fourth time.*

The signs in the heavens through the blood moons are not the only prophetic signs of things to come. The Bible also uses numbers in patterns to teach spiritual truths.

God precisely measures time on earth. In chapter 3 we will examine the prophecies of the past, which give us guidance into our immediate future in the Shemittah year, which occurs every seventh or every Sabbath year. God has an exact *set time* for all things to happen.

King David writes:

You will arise and have mercy on Zion [Israel];
For the time to favor her,
Yes, the set time, has come.

(PSALM 102:13)

CHAPTER 3

Warning Comes before Judgment

....

To whom shall I speak and give warning

That they may hear?

Behold, their ears are closed

And they cannot listen.

....

—JEREMIAH 6:10 NASB

Before we travel any further in our journey, allow me to define some terms I refer to often so you can better understand the prophetic message God is unveiling to His people.

LUNAR ECLIPSE

A lunar eclipse occurs when the earth's shadow blocks the sun's light, which otherwise reflects off the moon; the most dramatic is a total lunar eclipse. When the earth's shadow completely covers the moon it will turn *red* during the total portion of an eclipse.

BLOOD MOON

The *red moon* is possible because while the moon is in total shadow (total lunar eclipse), some light from the sun passes through the earth's atmosphere and is bent toward the moon. While other colors in the spectrum are blocked and scattered by earth's atmosphere, red light makes it through. Because of the moon's vivid color NASA scientists often refer to it as the Blood Red Moon.[1]

SOLAR ECLIPSE

A solar eclipse occurs when the moon comes between the earth and the sun, and the moon casts a shadow over earth. A solar eclipse can only take place at the phase of a new moon, when the moon passes directly between the sun and earth and its shadow falls upon earth's surface.[2]

The Bible clearly describes both blood moons and a solar eclipse in Joel 2:30–31 and Acts 2:19–20, and Jesus confirms them in Matthew 24:29 saying, "Immediately after the tribulation of those days the sun will be darkened and the moon will not give its light; the stars will fall from heaven and the powers of the heavens will be shaken."

TETRAD

A Tetrad is defined as four total lunar eclipses (Blood Moons) that consecutively occur during specific intervals of time. Lunar eclipses are relatively common, but total lunar eclipses are less common. A Tetrad is a rare occurrence and a Tetrad with a total solar eclipse within its series is even rarer. Furthermore, a Tetrad linked to Jewish history has only happened three times in the past five hundred-plus years—it's very rare![3]

THE ROMAN CALENDAR

The Roman or "pre-Julian" calendar was created during the founding of Rome and is believed to have been a lunar calendar. The calendar originally consisted of "hollow" months that were 29 days long or "full" months that had 30 days.

The original Roman calendar was said to be invented by Romulus, the first king of Rome, at around 753 BCE (Before Common Era). The calendar started the year in March (Martius) and consisted of 10 months, with 6 months of 30 days and 4 months of 31 days. The winter season was not assigned to any month, so the calendar year lasted only 304 days with 61 days unaccounted for in the winter.[4]

JULIAN CALENDAR

The Julian calendar was introduced by Julius Caesar and replaced the Roman calendar in 45 BCE. It has a regular (common) year of 365 days divided into 12 months with a leap day added to the month of February every four years (leap year), thus making the Julian year 365.25 days long on average.[5]

THE GREGORIAN CALENDAR

The Gregorian calendar is today's internationally accepted civil calendar and is also known as the "Western calendar" or "Christian calendar." It was named after Pope Gregory XIII, who first introduced it. It reformed the Julian calendar in 1582.

The calendar is strictly a solar calendar based on a 365-day common year, divided into 12 months of irregular lengths. Each month consists of either 30 or 31 days with 1 month consisting of 28 days during the common year.[6]

THE JEWISH CALENDAR

The Jewish calendar, also referred to as the Hebrew Calendar (Hebcal) is based on three astronomical phenomena: the rotation of the earth about its axis (a day); the revolution of the moon about the earth (a month); and the revolution of the earth about the sun (a year).

On average, the moon revolves around the earth in about 29.5 days. The earth revolves around the sun in about 365.25 days, that is, about 12.4 lunar months.

The Jewish calendar coordinates all three of these astronomical phenomena. The civil calendar used by most of the world has abandoned any correlation between the moon cycles and the month, but God's chosen people did not!

A BOOK OF SEVENS

The Bible is a book of very sophisticated and exact numbers. Take Genesis 1:1 as an example: "In the beginning God created the heavens and the earth."

Seven Hebrew words produce this sentence in English. There are twenty-eight Hebrew letters in those seven words. Four times seven equals twenty-eight. Four in Bible numerology represents the earth, and seven is the number of completion. Therefore, the mathematical message of Genesis 1:1 is that at the end of Genesis 1:1, God had created a perfect world.

The Bible is a book of sevens. There are seven days in creation. God worked six days and rested the seventh. Through this timetable God signified that there would be six days of one thousand years, and the seventh day of glorious and perfect rest called the Millennial Reign. Second Peter 3:8 confirms God's timetable: "With the Lord one day is as a thousand years, and a thousand years as one day."

Continue with the concept of the Bible being a book of sevens. The apostle John addresses the seven churches of Asia (Revelation 2–3). In the book of Revelation there are seven seals, seven trumpets, and seven vials pronouncing the Great Tribulation judgments.

There are:

- Seven days in the week (Genesis 2:2)
- Seven Ages and Dispensations (Genesis 1:3 through Revelation 21:1)

- 7 x 7 = 49; the year of Jubilee; a time of full restoration (Leviticus 25:8–12)
- 49 x 10 = 490; in the Bible God does something that changes the course of history every 490 years

Dr. Clarence Larkin presents a brilliant and extensive study of the theme of *sevens* in the Bible in his book, *Dispensational Truth.*

Larkin establishes the birth of Abraham as 2111 BC; 490 years (70 x 7) passed until the Exodus of the Israel from Egypt's bondage.[7]

The actual time was 505 years, but for fifteen years, according to Genesis 16:16 and Genesis 21:15, Abraham looked at Ishmael as the promised seed. It was, in fact, Isaac who was the promised seed. God did not count those fifteen years because the promised seed had not arrived. As I stated before, God establishes His own timetable.

From the Exodus to the dedication of Solomon's Temple was 490 years, as God counts time. The historical fact is that in this span of time God allowed Israel to be captured six times for a total of 111 years. When Israel is out of the land, God's timetable stops!

From the dedication of Solomon's Temple to the edict of Artaxerxes to rebuild the walls of Jerusalem was 490 years, not counting the seventy years Israel was in Babylonian captivity; again, when Israel is out of the land, God's timetable stops!

From the edict of Artaxerxes to the coming of Christ was 490 years. From AD 47 to AD 537 is 490 years; from AD 537 to AD 1027 is 490 years; from AD 1027 to AD 1517 is 490 years. As far as we know, these three spans of 490 year intervals from AD 47 to AD 1517 are silent in which nothing significant occurred. Their biblical value is to continue the 490 year chronology that takes us to the Reformation and the Turk's invasion of Israel, which occurred AD 1517.

God uses the number seven to measure time and judgments which brings us to the Shemittah year which happens every seven years.

The Shemittah Year

Shemittah is the Sabbatical year, which occurs every seventh year. *Shemittah* is "Shabbat" (the Sabbath) for the land of Israel; the land "rests" in a fashion, similar to the way the Jewish people rest every seventh day (Leviticus 25:4).

While *observing* Shemittah guarantees abundant produce, *neglecting* it leads to judgment. Jeremiah foretold that the Jewish people would be exiled for not keeping Shemittah by not allowing the land to rest (Jeremiah 17:4). When the Jewish people violated the law of Shemittah, God exiled them for seventy years until the land "enjoyed her Sabbaths" (2 Chronicles 36:19–21).

Jewish tradition teaches that exile is the penalty for the three cardinal sins of murder, idolatry, sexual immorality, *and* for neglecting to keep the laws of Shemittah! The next

Shemittah year occurs in 2015, which is also the appearance of the final Four Blood Moons that align with the Feasts of the Lord within this century.

AMERICA UNDER JUDGMENT

In America the judgment of violating Shemittah is not linked to the land of Israel but to our national disobedience to the Word of God. We give our allegiance to the idols of self-indulgence and greed, and our immorality is equivalent to that of Sodom and Gomorrah.

The year 2001 was a Shemittah year. What happened that year in America? On September 11, 2001, we were attacked for the first time on our soil since the British burned the White House in 1813. (The Japanese attack on Pearl Harbor occurred before Hawaii became a state of the Union.)

Radical Islamic terrorists came to our country and hijacked four commercial planes with box cutters and flew them into New York's Twin Towers, the Pentagon, and a field in Pennsylvania, killing nearly three thousand of our citizens and crushing the illusion that America would never be attacked on our soil by an invading foreign power. September 11, 2001, will forever be remembered as America's new Day of Infamy!

Add seven years to the year 2001, and you have the year 2008, another Shemittah year. What happened that year in America? The *Wall Street Journal* reported[8] that the economic collapse of the American economy began at the end of November 2007, the results of which became obvious and painfully real when the stock market collapsed *777* points on September 29, 2008.

What's next?

The next Shemittah year occurs in 2014–15, which takes place within the series of the next Four Blood Moons.

God always sends a nation warning before He sends judgment; are we listening?

Will America be at war? Will America's mountain of debt come crashing down, destroying the dollar? Will global terrorists attack our nation again with a force that will make 9/11 pale by comparison?

The attacks on the Twin Towers were on September 11, 2001.

The Wall Street crash was on September 29, 2008.

The next Tetrad will end in September 2015, which will include the Year of Shemittah. Will a crisis happen as before? What earthshaking event will it be?

This we know: things are about to change forever!

THE ABSOLUTE AUTHORITY OF PROPHECY

When discussing the signs of the times you want to find someone who is an absolute authority on Bible prophecy; someone who is always right and has never had to change his prophecy chart. Well, I have found that *Someone*. He is the Living Word!

He is the Word that "became flesh and dwelt among us":

> The Word became flesh and made his dwelling among us. We have seen his glory, the glory of the one and only Son, who came from the Father, full of grace and truth.
>
> (JOHN 1:14 NIV)

Jesus took His twelve disciples up the slopes of the Mount of Olives to give them the Spine of Prophecy—it was everything they needed to know from that moment until His glorious second coming.

The Spine of Prophecy is revealed in chapter 4.

SECTION 2

THE SPINE OF PROPHECY

CHAPTER 4
The Spine of Prophecy

O Jerusalem, Jerusalem, the one who kills the
prophets and stones those who are sent to her!
How often I wanted to gather your children together,
as a hen gathers her chicks under her wings,
but you were not willing!

—MATTHEW 23:37

The spinal column is the articulated series of thirty-three ver-
tebrae in the human body from the base of the skull to the tail-
bone. This is the support pillar of our divinely crafted physical
body. Let one vertebra become dislocated, and the body immediately begins to suffer. Let two become dislocated and the

body becomes incapacitated and surgery is required. In many ways the spine determines the health of the whole body.

That's the reason I have titled this seminal chapter "The Spine of Prophecy." As long as each prophetic vertebra is in place, it produces peace and confidence concerning our future and the future of the world. Let one element (vertebra) of prophecy get distorted and you begin to suffer spiritually. Let more than one element get dislocated and your theology is skewed needing a scriptural adjustment to correct.

Before we can fully grasp the significance of the coming Four Blood Moons, we must know and understand the spine of biblical prophecy concerning the end of the world as we know it. We will look closer at the twenty-fourth chapter of Matthew to reveal the blueprint of things to come.

The Author of Matthew 24 is the only Master Teacher of Prophecy who ever lived—Jesus Christ, the Son of God, the Son of David, our King, and our Redeemer. Let's join Jesus, the Rabbi, and the twelve disciples at His Prophecy Conference on the Mount of Olives.

THE PROPHECY CONFERENCE

In the theater of your mind, go back with me two thousand years as Jesus of Nazareth is leading His twelve disciples out of the majestic Temple of Jerusalem toward the Mount of Olives.

They cross the Kidron Valley and start to climb the rocky slopes of the Mount, which is studded with ancient olive trees that have witnessed biblical prophecy unfold through the ages. As they climb toward a clearing of trees, the mood is somber for the disciples are beginning to feel that their future is uncertain.

Jesus sits on a large boulder under the shade of a massive tree as a cool spring breeze blows His hair away from His face. The Master is sitting on the very place where the prophet Zechariah had predicted that the Messiah would stand when He came to establish His eternal kingdom (14:4).

The disciples gather closely; this is the moment Jesus has chosen to share the future with them—the very Spine of Prophecy.

The Twelve were filled with gut-twisting anxiety because Jesus had clearly told them that He was going to die (Matthew 16:21; 17:23; 20:18–19). The disciples had been certain that Jesus would establish an eternal kingdom *now* and that they were going to sit on twelve thrones judging the twelve tribes of Israel *now* (Matthew 19:28–29)!

What did Jesus' foreboding declaration mean?

The disciples were so certain the glorious kingdom was going to come about in *their* lifetime that two of them had their mother lobby Jesus for preferment so that one could sit on His right hand (the position of power) and the other on His left.

When Jesus informed the determined mother that He was going to die, the rabid enthusiasm among His ambitious disciples immediately diminished to an all-time low. They were looking for diadems—not death!

To make the mood even worse, Jesus had recently blistered the Jewish leaders by publicly calling them "hypocrites" (Matthew 23:13). Jesus said to the scribes and Pharisees that their converts were "twice as much a son of hell as yourselves" (v. 15). He accused them of being "fools and blind" (vv. 17, 19) and "blind guides, who strain out a gnat and swallow a camel" (v. 24).

This scorching sermon directed at Israel's elite established religious order continued with Jesus pointing His forefinger in their ashen faces and saying, "You cleanse the outside of the cup and dish, but inside they are full of extortion and self-indulgence" (v. 25). He called them "whitewashed tombs . . . full of dead men's bones (v. 27), guilty of "shedding the blood of the prophets" like their forefathers (v. 30–31 NASB). Jesus said to them, "Serpents, brood of vipers! How can you escape the condemnation of hell?" (v. 33). Obviously Jesus didn't read the book *How to Win Friends and Influence People.*

There was no organ playing "Just as I Am" in the background, and Jesus wasn't asking for hands to be raised for those convicted of sin. No one was taking photos for His monthly miracle magazine. Jesus was not wearing a six-inch diamond-studded cross around His neck and a pinkie ring on his finger. There was no limo lurking in the shadows to speed Him away from His adoring audience.

The truth is . . . Jesus was so common in His appearance that Judas had to kiss Him to identify Him to the Roman soldiers in the Garden of Gethsemane. The scribes and the Pharisees were flooded with rage at this rogue Rabbi from Nazareth who dared to question their holiness and condemn their unlimited pomposity and offend their endless religious pride.

This same religious pride continues today as the sermons of many twenty-first-century clergy have become more a mixture of pop psychology and psychobabble than the pure preaching of the gospel. Their purpose is to make the hearers *feel good* instead of challenging them to *do good*. These modern day messengers are more concerned about their reputation than winning souls; they need to catch the spirit of Jesus recorded in the book of Matthew.

SATAN'S SNARE

"From pride, vainglory, and hypocrisy; from envy, hatred, and malice, and from all want of charity, Good Lord, deliver us."[1]

Pride is Satan's snare!

The spirit that caused Adam and Eve to sin against God was pride; they would rather point fingers at one another than repent of their disobedience. The spirit that caused Cain to murder Abel was pride. The spirit that caused Israel to follow other gods was pride. And the spirit that sent Jesus to the cross . . . that lurked in the heart of every Pharisee . . . was the spirit of self-righteous pride.

That same demonic spirit is destroying America; it deceives us in believing that we know how to run our lives and lead our nation better than God can. America is going the wrong way, and in our vainglorious pride we have refused to change direction.

> Pride goes before destruction,
> And a haughty spirit before a fall.
>
> (PROVERBS 16:18)

Pride is the swelling in a heart filled with self-importance. Pride lifts *me* up so I can look down on *you*. Pride is a spiritual cancer that devours families, destroys marriages, divides churches, and corrupts governments. Pride is what makes half of our country's leadership look in the mirror every morning and sing "Hail to the Chief"!

Pride is rooted in idolatry—you worship yourself. You don't need your wife, your husband, or your children. You don't even need God . . . because in your world *you* are God!

Pride is a poisonous weed that grows in all soils without need of water or care. It consumes and kills everything it touches.

But for pride, the angels who are in hell would be in heaven.

But for pride, Nebuchadnezzar, who ate grass in the forest with cows, could have been in his royal palace.

But for pride, the Pharisees would have received Jesus Christ as freely as His disciples—but the piercing words of the Nazarene cut the pompous religious leaders to the bone, and they began to plot the murder of the Son of God! Don't ever forget: Jesus was murdered by the pride of the self-righteous religious leaders of the recognized church in Jerusalem.

Pride is a cancer that kills everything and everyone it touches. Is it in your church? Is it in your family? Is it in you? Get it out now! Your very spiritual survival is at stake.

America is ensnared in self-indulgence and its future hangs in the balance. Our moral and spiritual foundations are rapidly being destroyed. Our arrogance is producing a socialist state that is becoming our god. The entitlement *state* of mind has created a nation that looks to the government for the answer to our problems, when the only answer is, "Our Father which art in heaven."

The majority of Americans are *voting* for a living rather than *working* for a living. Work is God's idea! God worked six days in creation and, in the Ten Commandments, commanded all men to work six days. In our arrogant pride we are telling Almighty God, "We don't need You."

Wake up, America, we are going in the wrong direction!

THE ROMANS' DESTRUCTION OF THE TEMPLE

As Jesus continued His Prophecy Conference He pointed toward the magnificent Temple, and said: "Do you not see all these things? Assuredly, I say to you, 'not one stone shall be left here upon another, that shall not be thrown down'" (Matthew 24:2).

This one statement from the Master was a dream killer for the Twelve. If this glorious Temple that took forty-six years to build was going to be torn down stone by massive stone by an invading army, there was no glorious kingdom in their future.

I have traveled to Israel thirty-five times and each time I have seen the only surviving wall of the Roman siege—the Western Wall of the Temple. The stones in that wall, according to our guides, weigh as much as four hundred tons; these stones are impressive indeed.

Exactly as Jesus had prophesied, the Temple was destroyed when the Romans seized Jerusalem just four years after it was completed. The invasion of the Roman army destroyed more than the Temple; according to the historian Josephus, approximately one million Jews were killed or died from starvation during that Roman massacre.[2] The Jewish inhabitants of Jerusalem that survived this vicious siege fled and dispersed to the nations of the world, which began what history calls the Diaspora.

As the disciples gazed at this massive structure, they found Jesus' words about its destruction impossible to believe. But on the 9th of Av, a date that proved over and over to be infamous in the history of the Jewish people, the Temple was no more.

Day of Tragedy—the 9th of Av

Av is the fifth month of the Jewish year.[3] *The 9th of Av* is a day of infamy for the Jewish people for many tragedies have befallen them on this doomful day. It proves beyond any reasonable doubt that history *does* repeat itself. Let us review some of the significant Jewish tragedies that occurred on the 9th of Av:

- The children of Israel refused to enter the Promised Land, causing that generation to die in the wilderness (Numbers 14).
- The Temple was destroyed for the first time (423 BC).
- The Temple was destroyed a second time (AD 69).
- Pope Urban II declared the first Crusade (1095 CE).
- The Jewish people were expelled from England (AD 1290).
- The Jewish people were expelled from Spain (1492).
- The gas chambers of Treblinka began to operate in Poland (1942).

Is this concidental, or will history repeat itself?

CHAPTER 5

When Will These Things Be?

Now as He sat on the Mount of Olives, the disciples
came to Him privately, saying, "Tell us, when will
these things be? And what will be the sign of Your
coming, and of the end of the age?"

—Matthew 24:3

The twelve disciples are now getting the picture—Jesus is going to be killed, just as He said. There would be no glorious
kingdom in their lifetime where they would rule from twelve
thrones. The Temple would be destroyed, and the nation of
Israel scattered.

So what was to come?

The disciples asked three questions to clarify the future of Israel and the Jewish people:

1. "Tell us, when will these things be?"
2. "What will be the sign of Your coming?"
3. "[What are the signs] of the end of the age?"

The "end of the age" is the second coming of Christ—not the rapture of the church. Many are now asking what signs must be fulfilled before the church can be raptured from the earth. The answer is *zero*! The Rapture of the church of Jesus Christ is imminent; it could happen before you finish reading this page.

The theological opinions about Matthew 24 are as numerous as the stars in the sky. I am presenting Matthew 24 from the position of a premillennialist, which means I believe Jesus Christ will come for His church in an event called the *Rapture* before the seven years of the Great Tribulation, led by the Antichrist.

Following the Great Tribulation will be the second coming of Christ according to Revelation 19:11–16. Christ will return to this earth followed by the armies that are in heaven. He will destroy the enemies of Israel that have come against them in the Battle of Armageddon. He will return to the Mount of Olives, then cross the Kidron Valley and enter the Eastern Gate of the city of Jerusalem, where He will set up His eternal kingdom on the Temple Mount, and of His kingdom there shall be no end.

Jesus was giving the Spine of Prophecy primarily to the Jewish people. I am presenting Matthew 24:1–14 as general signs of His return; remember, this is a *Jewish* rabbi speaking to twelve *Jewish* disciples about the future of the *Jewish* people. Matthew 24:15 and the verses following record specific signs of His second coming.

ROMAN DESTRUCTION OF JERUSALEM

Jesus looked into the bewildered faces of His disciples and warned them that in the immediate future an invading army would surround and destroy the sacred city of Jerusalem.

> So when you see standing in the holy place "the abomination that causes desolation," spoken of through the prophet Daniel—let the reader understand—then let those who are in Judea flee to the mountains.
>
> (MATTHEW 24:15–16 NIV)

The disciples thought on the words of the prophet Daniel who prophesied about Jerusalem's coming desolation (9:27). He also foretold of Jerusalem's attack by four world empires: the Babylonians, the Medo-Persians, the Greeks under Alexander the Great and, lastly, the Romans (Daniel 2:31–45).

I can only imagine what this horrific news meant to the disciples. These men were looking at a thriving city where the

Temple was the focal point of their society. How could this beautiful city be destroyed?

However unbelievable; Jerusalem's destruction came to pass.

Josephus—the Historian

Josephus was a priest, a soldier, and a historical scholar who was born in Jerusalem in 37 CE, a few years after the time of Jesus and during the time of the Roman occupation of the Jewish homeland. Josephus, a witness to the destruction of the city of Jerusalem and the Holy Temple, chronicled the events of the war.

In his writings Josephus recorded horrific scenes such as mothers eating their infant children who had died of starvation. The list below notes some of the entries made in Josephus' account of the siege and destruction of Jerusalem from March through September AD 70:

- After the Roman siege began, Jewish citizens sold their possessions for gold and then swallowed the gold coins to hide them as they escaped the Romans. The rumor spread that all deserters were filled with gold. Arabs and Syrians cut open all who escaped the city. "In one night no less than two thousand were ripped up."
- The Romans captured escapees from the city, as many as 500 a day. Prisoners were tortured, crucified, and

killed to intimidate the populace. Titus is quoted as saying, "So great was their number, that space could not be found for the crosses nor crosses for the bodies."

- Titus blockaded the city to prevent food supplies from entering. With all hope of escape cut off, the famine within the city intensified. Burials were neglected and the bodies piled up.

- Prisoner Mannaeus ben Lazarus was assigned by the Romans to watch a city gate. He counted 115,880 bodies carried through the gate during the siege. Reports from within the city gave the total dead among the lower classes at 600,000.

- The victims of famine were dying in countless numbers. Starving men like mad dogs staggered from house to house searching for food. Shoe leather and grass was gnawed on.

- Josephus provided an eyewitness account of the destruction, the fire, and the noise. "You would indeed have thought that the Temple-hill was boiling over from its base, being everywhere one mass of flame, yet the stream of blood was more copious than the flames." He observed that this was on the very day and month that the First Temple had been burnt by the Babylonians; it was the 9th of Av.

- Romans carried standards (symbols of their gods) into the Temple and made sacrifices unto them.

- The Romans commanded the whole city, planted standards on the walls, and looted the city. All Jerusalem was in flames.
- Titus ordered the whole city and Temple to be razed to the ground, leaving only the tallest towers and a small portion of the wall on the west.

This horror was prophesied by Jesus as He carried His cross through the streets of Jerusalem and saw the Jewish mothers weeping over His crucifixion.

> Daughters of Jerusalem, do not weep for Me, but weep for yourselves and for your children. For indeed the days are coming in which they will say, "Blessed are the barren, wombs that never bore, and breasts which never nursed!"
>
> (LUKE 23:28–29)

Jesus saw the future! He saw the Roman legions surrounding Jerusalem to destroy the Holy City and the Temple. He saw the unspeakable horror and mind-bending tragedy inflicted by General Titus and the Roman Tenth Legion in AD 70.

When the Romans destroyed Jerusalem, the first part of the Olivet Discourse was fulfilled.

JERUSALEM—THE CITY OF GOD

Jerusalem is not like any other city on earth; the world revolves around Jerusalem. Jerusalem is the city of God! "The LORD has chosen Zion; He has desired it for His dwelling place" (Psalm 132:13).

> Great is the LORD, and greatly to be praised
> In the city of our God,
> In His holy mountain.
> Beautiful in elevation,
> The joy of the whole earth
> Is Mount Zion . . .
> The city of our God:
> God will establish it *forever*.
>
> (PSALM 48:1–2, 8)

Jerusalem *is* where Abraham placed Isaac on an altar to sacrifice him, proving Abraham's love and loyalty to God Almighty. Centuries later on this same mountain, Jesus Christ was bound to the cross by the will of God His Father, and He sacrificed His life for our redemption. This was the absolute fulfillment of Abraham's words—"Jehovah Jireh"—meaning "The LORD will provide" (Genesis 22:12–14).

Jerusalem is where Jeremiah and Isaiah penned the principles of righteousness, which became the moral and spiritual foundations of Western civilization.

Jerusalem was conquered by King David three thousand years ago as he and his mighty men of valor drove out the occultic Jebusites. Jerusalem is once again the eternal and un-divided capital of the nation of Israel, and may it ever be.

> If I forget you, O Jerusalem,
> Let my right hand forget its skill!
> If I do not remember you,
> Let my tongue cling to the roof of my mouth—
> If I do not exalt Jerusalem
> Above my chief joy.
>
> (PSALM 137:5–6)

In these verses, David is attempting to describe his com-plete devotion to the City of God. David was willing to sacri-fice his life as a psalmist if he forgot to praise his beloved city, for at that point, life for him would have no meaning.

Jerusalem was the city where Jesus was circumcised in the Temple on the eighth day and where He celebrated His bar mitzvah on His thirteenth birthday. It is where He celebrat-ed His last Passover with the Twelve in the upper room, and where He was betrayed by Judas.

Jerusalem was the city where He was arrested, tried, and convicted as the result of a Roman conspiracy between the Pharisees and the High Priest.

Jerusalem was where He was beaten with thirty-nine

stripes and was crowned with thorns while Roman spittle dripped off His holy face onto the purple robe of mockery placed upon His blood-soaked back.

Just outside the walls of Jerusalem was where Jesus Christ was crucified with thieves for our redemption. Jerusalem was where Jesus died for our sins.

Jerusalem was where He rose from a borrowed grave and became the firstfruits of the resurrection. Because He lives we shall also live. Hallelujah!

As we will see in the coming chapters, Jerusalem will be attacked by the Antichrist (Zechariah 14:1–2). But this time the Lion of the tribe of Judah will triumph over all of Jerusalem's enemies.

Most importantly, Jerusalem is the city where Jesus will return. He will rule from Jerusalem. When Messiah, the Son of David, Jesus Christ of Nazareth, the Lamb of God, sits on His holy throne, the nations of the world, including *you and I*, will go to Jerusalem to keep the Feast of Tabernacles (Zechariah 14:16–18).

> The moon will be dismayed,
> the sun ashamed;
> for the LORD Almighty will reign
> on Mount Zion and in Jerusalem,
> and before its elders—with great glory.
>
> (ISAIAH 24:23 NIV)

Jerusalem will remain the center of the universe for the future of the world!

CHAPTER 6
Concerning the Rapture

The Lord Himself will descend from heaven with a shout,
with the voice of an archangel, and with the trumpet of
God. And the dead in Christ will rise first. Then we who
are alive and remain shall be caught up together with
them *in the clouds* to meet the Lord in the air.

—1 THESSALONIANS 4:16–17

Jesus warned His disciples that deception would prevail before His return. His disciples were grappling with the reality
that there was no glorious kingdom coming in their lifetimes
and that this miracle-working Nazarene was going to die like
any ordinary man. Rome was all powerful *after all*!

Satan is the master of deception. He presents himself as an angel of light, when in fact he is the prince of darkness. A prince is one who has limited authority in a specific kingdom. There are only two kingdoms: the kingdom of light and the kingdom of darkness. You are in one of these kingdoms right now.

Satan has authority in the kingdom of darkness, and his mission is "to steal, and to kill, and to destroy" you and those you love (John 10:10). The only way out of the kingdom of darkness is to accept Jesus Christ, the Light of the World, as your Savior and Lord.

The authority of the kingdom of darkness is broken by the spoken Word of God, which is a divine proclamation based on Scripture. The Bible says, "And they overcame him [Satan] by the blood of the Lamb and by the word of their testimony [proclamation]" (Revelation 12:11).

Satan, the master of deception, comes as a wolf in sheep's clothing. He and his messengers present themselves as meek and humble, but their end objective is your destruction. Satan is a deadly serpent who is the master of disguise. He can lie in the brush unseen and unnoticed, totally and perfectly camouflaged, appearing completely harmless until his razor-sharp fangs are embedded deep into your flesh and his deadly venom is surging through your veins.

Satan's deception is rampant in this twenty-first century. We are the generation that must have a lawyer in one hand

and an accountant in the other to "trust but verify." Who believes the promises of a politician when he is speaking? The generation where every man's word was his bond is dead.

Jesus gave this warning to His disciples because when the Antichrist appears during the Tribulation period it will be a day of deception. The Antichrist will come as a prince of peace, yet he will bathe the world in blood. He will make treaties he has no intention of keeping. He will present himself as an economic czar and prove to be a global dictator.

Peter warns the church in 2 Peter 2:1:

There will be false teachers among you, who will secretly bring in destructive heresies, even denying the Lord who bought them, and bring on themselves swift destruction.

There are false prophets today who have abandoned traditional values for the message of political correctness. Their message and motive is to make people feel good without being good, to master the ritual without achieving righteousness, and to conform to their sin without confessing their sin.

They have forgotten the mandate from the apostle Paul to "preach the Word" (2 Timothy 4:2). They have forgotten these immortal words of Dietrich Bonhoeffer, the Lutheran pastor whose passion for truth drove him to confront Adolf Hitler and Germany:

Silence in the face of evil is itself evil. God will not hold us guiltless. Not to speak is to speak. Not to act is to act.[1]

America is filled with false prophets. Any person presenting the gospel of Jesus Christ who does not teach or preach the literal Word of God is a false prophet. I encourage you to "recognize those who labor among you" (1 Thessalonians 5:12) and refuse to follow, in any manner, those wolves in sheep's clothing who are masters of deception in our generation.

Some of these false prophets are now teaching there will be no Rapture of the church! What does God's Word say? Why is it extremely important for you to know the truth about this doctrine?

THE TRUTH—THE RAPTURE IS COMING

Jesus told His disciples on the Mount of Olives:

Watch therefore, and pray always that you may be counted worthy to escape all these things that will come to pass, and to stand before the Son of Man.

(LUKE 21:36)

The point is very clear: if you are not watching for His coming, you will not be counted "worthy to escape all the things that will come to pass" during the Great Tribulation. If you're not watching for *Him,* He's not coming for *you*!

If you are deceived into believing there is no Rapture, prepare to stand in line to get your personal tattoo from the Antichrist. If you refuse his marking, he will cut off your head! Are you interested in hearing about the Rapture now?

The apostle Paul makes it unmistakably clear that if you're not looking for Jesus, you're not going with Him in the Rapture. He writes:

> To those who eagerly wait for Him He will appear a second time.
>
> (HEBREWS 9:28)

If Jesus is coming back, why now? The Bible says:

> Scoffers will come in the last days, walking according to their own lusts, and saying, "Where is the promise of His coming?' For since the fathers fell asleep, all things continue as they were from the beginning of creation.
>
> (2 PETER 3:3–4)

The fact that men do not believe Christ is coming back is living proof and biblical evidence that the Rapture of the church is imminent. If you listen closely you can hear the footsteps of Messiah . . . tiptoeing through the clouds of heaven.

Get ready! The King is coming!

Paul describes the Rapture to the believers in Corinth and Thessalonika by declaring:

1. "For the [last] trumpet will sound . . ." (1 Corinthians 15:52) and "The Lord Himself will descend from heaven with a shout . . ." (1 Thessalonians 4:16).
2. "We will not all sleep, but we will all be changed—" (1 Corinthians 15:51) and "The dead in Christ will rise first . . ." (1 Thessalonians 4:16).
3. "In the twinkling of an eye . . . the dead shall be raised . . ." (1 Corinthians 15:52) and "Then we who are alive and remain shall be caught up together with them *in the clouds* to meet the Lord in the air" (1 Thessalonians 4:17).

Have men been taken into heaven before their death? The answer is yes . . . *twice!*

Enoch, the father of Jared "walked faithfully with God; then he was no more, because God took him away" (Genesis 5:24 NIV).

The prophet Elijah was carried into heaven in a chariot of fire (2 Kings 2:11). He has been there for thousands of years and will return to earth during the Great Tribulation as God's messenger to the Jewish people announcing to them that Messiah is coming!

Think also of Jesus Christ, who went into heaven forty days after He rose from the dead. He ascended into heaven from the Mount of Transfiguration in full view of His disciples. He arose on the 16th of Nisan, which is the Feast of First Fruits. In His resurrection, He is the firstfruits of the millions who will be raptured in the church.

The following verse paints this picture—Jesus Christ, the Prince of Glory, appearing suddenly in the heavens:

> Men of Galilee, why do you stand gazing up into heaven? This same Jesus, who was taken up from you into heaven, will so come in like manner as you saw Him go into heaven.
>
> (ACTS 1:11)

When the time comes, the trumpet of God shall sound, announcing the appearance of royalty, for He is the Prince of Peace, the King of kings and the Lord of lords. He is coming in the clouds of heaven for those who are watching for His glorious appearing. Look up, my friends, for the King is coming!

THE REAL JESUS

If you don't believe in the Rapture as described in the Bible, where believers rise to meet the Lord in the air, how will you know when the real Jesus comes to earth?

Anyone can stand on the Mount of Olives and say, "I'm Jesus." Anyone can wear a white robe and claim to be a descendant of King David. Anyone can have his followers crown him as the king of the "New Israel" on the Temple Mount in Jerusalem. Anyone can surgically have scars placed in his hands and feet. Even the False Prophet of the Antichrist will cause a statue to speak and perform other miracles at his bidding.

This is not the real Jesus! He's an imposter! A fraud! This is satanic deception—which Jesus spoke about in Matthew 24:5 and 11.

God knew from the beginning that imposters and frauds would come and claim to be Christ, deceiving many, "if possible, even the elect" (Matthew 24:24). Jesus said, "If anyone says to you, 'Look, here is the Christ,' or 'There!' do not believe it" (v. 23).

On one occasion a church member told me, "Pastor, a lady said she was driving in California, and suddenly Jesus appeared in the car with her. What do you think?"

"I'll tell you what I think: I believe it not!"

Jesus Christ is not in California, New York, or Rome. He is seated at the right hand of God the Father—where He will stay until Gabriel blows the trumpet to call the dead in Christ from their dusty couches of slumber to mansions of splendor in heaven.

Jesus knew that many "false christs" would come, saying, "I am the Christ" and will deceive many (Matthew 24:5).

A FAILSAFE STRATEGY

God installed a *failsafe strategy* in Scripture that is so staggering in supernatural power, so earth shattering by design, that not even Satan and his demonic legions could imitate it, much less duplicate it.

That failsafe strategy is the rapture of the church!

Satan tries to replicate whatever God does. He disguises himself as an *angel of light* emulating Jesus Christ who is the Light of the World (2 Corinthians 11:14). In Revelation 6, the Antichrist rides out onto the stage of world history on a *white horse* as the "prince of peace" who will plunge the world into the bloodiest war in history. He does so because Jesus returns to earth riding a white horse in the book of Revelation (19:11).

The Antichrist will be shot in the head and will *recover miraculously* (Revelation 13:3), imitating the death and resurrection of Jesus Christ.

Satan hates the Rapture teaching and has his deluded disciples saying there will be no Rapture. The rapture is Christ's celebration over death, hell, and the grave which He defeated when He died on the cross. It is the ultimate humiliation of Satan.

How will you know when the real Jesus gets here?

Not by what you read in the *New York Times* or by what some Ivy League theologian says, not by some charismatic personality standing on the Mount of Olives in a white bed sheet saying he is the king of the New Israel, and not by a warlock calling fire from heaven.

You will know it's the real Jesus when your body sails

through the air past the Milky Way a million miles a minute; you will know when you stand in His glorious presence with your brand-new, disease-proof body.

When you stand in His presence with your transfigured body, your fatigue-free body, your pain-free body, and your never-dying body, you'll know it's the real Jesus and this is the real heaven.

THE BIBLE: LITERAL OR ALLEGORICAL?

Those attacking the Rapture are teaching that the Bible is not literal, that it's allegorical or a myth. If the Bible is a myth, then I'm *myth-taken, myth-tified,* and of all men most *myth-erable!* The Bible is literal from cover to cover:

- God Almighty literally created the "heavens and the earth." (Genesis 1:1)
- Jesus was literally born of a virgin named Mary. (Luke 1:34)
- He was literally born in Bethlehem, Israel. (Matthew 2:1)
- He literally healed the sick, diseased, the blind, the lame, and the leper instantly. (Matthew 4:23; Mark 10:52; Luke 7:22; John 5:8)
- He literally died on the cross. (Mark 15:22–32; Matthew 27:33–44; Luke 23:33–43; John 19:17–24)
- He literally was buried in a borrowed grave. (Matthew 27:57–61; Mark 15:42–47; Luke 23:50–56; John 19:38–42)
- He literally rose from the dead and was seen by five

hundred plus people in thirteen different places. (John 21:14; Mark 16:14; Acts 1:1–13)

- He literally sits at the right hand of God the Father. (Hebrews 12:2; 1 Peter 3:22)
- We are literally going to rise to meet Him in the air in the twinkling of an eye. (1 Corinthians 15:52)
- He literally is coming back again with power and great glory, and: "Every knee should bow . . . every tongue should confess that Jesus Christ is Lord, to the glory of God the Father" (Philippians 2:10–11).
- We are literally going to walk on streets of gold. (Revelation 21:21)
- We are literally going to wear a crown of life. (Revelation 2:10)
- We are literally going to live forever and forever in God's tomorrow. (Revelation 13:6)

CAUGHT UP TOGETHER

Critics of the Rapture claim that, "The Rapture does not exist because the word *Rapture* does not appear in the biblical text." True, the specific word *Rapture* is not mentioned in Scripture; however, the Bible is a book of concepts and word pictures, so simple that a person of modest comprehension can grasp its truth.

The biblical text does not have the word *Trinity*, but repeatedly the Scripture refers to "the Father, Son, and the Holy Spirit."

The concept of the Trinity is very clear within the context of Scripture.

In Genesis we have the first hint of the Blessed Trinity, a plurality of Persons in the Godhead.[2] Later in Genesis 1:26, God said: "Let *Us* make man in *Our* image." "Our image" refers to God the Father, the Son, and the Holy Spirit.

The Trinity is also seen during Jesus' baptism:

When He had been baptized, Jesus came up immediately from the water; and behold, the heavens were
open to Him, and He saw the Spirit of God descending
like a dove and alighting upon Him. And suddenly a
voice came from heaven, saying, "This is My beloved
Son, in whom I am well pleased."

(MATTHEW 3:16–17)

Notice the depiction of the Trinity in this Scripture setting: Jesus the Son is in the water being baptized; the dove,
representing the Holy Spirit, is descending from heaven and
the voice speaking from heaven is God the Father, extending
His blessing upon His Son.

Matthew 28:19 also refers to the Trinity: "Go therefore and
make disciples of all nations, baptizing them in the name of the
Father and of the Son and of the Holy Spirit [three in one]."

Just as these examples depict the Trinity, 1 Corinthians 15:51–52 and 1 Thessalonians 14:16–17 are clear word

pictures of the Rapture of the church of Jesus Christ.

STAY ON THE ALERT

Although Christians like to debate about when the Lord will come, Scripture is clear that the Lord expects us to be on the alert for the time He is coming in the clouds to take his bride to heaven. Why? The answer is in the Word of God.

> But keep on the alert at all times, praying that you may have strength to escape all these things that are about to take place, and to stand before the Son of Man.
>
> (LUKE 21:36 NASB)

> So remember what you have received and heard; and keep it, and repent. Therefore if you do not wake up, I will come like a thief, and you will not know at what hour I will come to you.
>
> (REVELATION 3:3 NASB)

Jesus Christ is telling us to stay on the *alert* and to *wake up*! Because if we are not watching for His return, we will miss His coming and will not escape the future horrors of the Antichrist, and we will not receive the crown of life.

> . . . in a flash, in the twinkling of an eye, at the last trumpet. For the trumpet will sound, the dead will be

raised imperishable, and we will be changed.

(1 Corinthians 15:52)

"The Lord Himself will descend from heaven with a shout" and summon the righteous from their graves with the sound of the trump. All over the earth, tombs will explode as the occupants soar into the heavens; headstones and marble mausoleums will topple as the bodies of resurrected saints rise to meet the Lord at the meeting in the air (1 Thessalonians 4:16–17).

When that time comes, cars will suddenly stand empty beside freeways and highways, their motors running with drivers and occupants strangely missing. Homes of believers will have the dishes on the table; the food will be on the stove in preparation of the meal, but the tenants will have gone to the marriage supper of the Lamb.

Headlines will be screaming in bold type: "Millions Are Missing." "Christians Have Disappeared from the Earth." "Global Economic Crash Is Coming!"

TV cameras will go to the cemeteries around the world broadcasting empty graves and shattered mausoleums. They will show abandoned homes in suburban neighborhoods, the vacant high rise apartments in the world's cities, and tractors running aimlessly across acres of planting fields because the Christian farmers are gone!

All Christians will have been caught up heading to mansions on high!

Phone lines will be jammed with families trying to "reach out and touch someone" but their long distance service won't reach that far! People will be screaming into their smartphones, "Can you hear me now?"

Churches all over the world will be packed with weeping, sobbing, and hysterical people. Their friends and loved ones will suddenly be gone, and they will be left behind to go through the living hell of the Great Tribulation.[3]

When that happens, the chaos on earth will be failsafe evidence that Christ has removed His church from the planet. The salt and light of the earth will be gone. The restraint of the Holy Spirit will be removed and Satan and the demons of hell will rule the earth for seven years of unspeakable horror and bloodshed.

THE LAST TRUMP

There are some who, because of their interpretation of 1 Corinthians 15:51–52, teach that the church will go through the Tribulation.

> Behold, I tell you a mystery: We shall not all sleep [in death], but we shall all be changed—in a moment, in the twinkling of an eye, at *the last trumpet*.

The confusion comes with the phrase "the last trumpet." The only Bible passage that describes a series of trumpets is in

Revelation, where seven trumpets announce seven judgments coming on the earth.

Those in confusion interpret that the Rapture will happen after the seventh trumpet sounds, since it's the last trumpet in a series of trumpets. This interpretation is in error.

The *first trumpet* (shofar) sound recorded in the Bible was at Mount Sinai, where the children of Israel received the Ten Commandments (Exodus 19:16):

> On the morning of the third day there was thunder and lightning, with a thick cloud over the mountain, and a very loud trumpet blast. Everyone in the camp trembled.

The *last trump* is recorded in 1 Corinthians 15:52, when the church is raptured:

> Listen, I tell you a mystery: We will not all sleep, but we will all be changed—in a flash, in the twinkling of an eye, at the last trumpet. For the trumpet will sound, the dead will be raised imperishable, and we will be changed.

The *great trump* is blown at the second coming of Jesus Christ, as recorded in Matthew 24:30–31:

> Then will appear the sign of the Son of Man in heaven.

And then all the peoples of the earth will mourn when they see the Son of Man coming on the clouds of heaven, with power and great glory. And he will send his angels with a loud trumpet call, and they will gather his elect from the four winds, from one end of the heavens to the other.

We are commanded to "watch," which means we must know the Spine of Prophecy and diligently look for God's announcements in the heavens through signs such as the Four Blood Moons. The Bible is clear that only those who "watch" will be counted worthy to escape those things that are coming on the earth.

Exactly what are we going to escape?

THE TRIBULATION

Those that are "taken up" in the Rapture will escape the wrath of the Antichrist. The Tribulation begins with the four horsemen of the Apocalypse appearing in Revelation 6. The first rider is the Antichrist, riding a white horse and coming to conquer the nations of the world.

He will make a seven-year peace treaty with Israel and break it after only three and a half years; he will cause every person on earth to receive his mark on their right hand or forehead, and without it you cannot buy or sell. Those who reject his mark will have their heads cut off (Revelation 13:16).

The monster on the white horse will put together a world government, a New World Order that will have ten kingdoms, which he will initially rule. The Antichrist will receive his power directly from Satan; he is the "son of perdition" (John 17:12; 2 Thessalonians 2:3), which means the chief son of Satan.

He will conquer three of these ten kingdoms, and the final form of the New World Order will be a kingdom with seven heads and ten crowns described by the prophet Daniel.

UNSPEAKABLE SUFFERING

In addition to the Antichrist (the Beast of Revelation), the Tribulation will bring global wars that will bathe the earth in blood (Matthew 24:6), earthquakes that will reshape the earth as mountains are reduced to rubble (v. 7) and the islands of the sea will disappear beneath the water (Psalm 46:2).

The sun will become so hot that the vegetation of the earth will be burned up; the oceans will be turned to blood and the waters of earth will be as bitter as wormwood, bringing death to those who drink it (Revelation 8:11).

Locusts the size of a horse will be released from the bottomless pit for five months and will be given power to sting men with venom that causes excruciating pain (Revelation 9:5).

In Revelation 9:15, four angels are released by God Almighty to destroy one-third of mankind in one day. In America that is the equivalent to one hundred million people in one twenty-four-hour period. In the world that would mean two billion people. It's absolutely mind-boggling.

Just how bad will it get? John, the Revelator pulls back the curtain of time and allows us to look into the abyss of unspeakable suffering:

> The kings of the earth, the great men, the rich men, the commanders, the mighty men, every slave and every free man, hid themselves in the caves and in the rocks of the mountains, and said to the mountains and rocks, "Fall on us and hide us from the face of Him who sits on the throne and from the wrath of the Lamb! For the great day of His wrath has come, and who is able to stand?"
>
> (REVELATION 6:15–18)

I ask those of you who are of sound mind, do you want to escape these horrors that John the Revelator so graphically described? I do! I really do! I am going to escape, in a moment, in the twinkling of an eye, at the last trump!

I'll literally rise into the heavens with millions of believers, to meet the real Jesus. I will walk on literal streets of gold and live in very real mansions of splendor with the bride of Christ . . . and so shall we ever be with the Lord!

You will either bow before the Antichrist or bow before Jesus Christ. It's not a matter of *if* you will bow; it's just a matter of *when* you will bow.

Has the Rapture Happened?

The deception that Jesus warned us about in Matthew 24 is spreading in our generation like a contagious theological virus with lies such as Jesus has already returned and the rapture of the church is a thing of the past. Not so! In fact, Paul writes about those "who have wandered away from the truth. They say that the resurrection has already taken place, and they destroy the faith of some" (2 Timothy 2:18).

Peter declares:

We did not follow cunningly devised fables when we made known to you the power and coming of our Lord Jesus Christ, but were *eyewitnesses* of His majesty.

(2 Peter 1:16)

The question is: when did Simon Peter see the power and coming of Jesus Christ? Peter makes it clear he is referring to the transfiguration of Christ. He continues:

He received from God the Father honor and glory when such a voice came to Him from the Excellent Glory: "This is My beloved Son, in whom I am well pleased." And we heard this voice which came from heaven when we were with Him on *the holy mountain*.

(vv. 17–18)

When Peter speaks of "the holy mountain," he is referring to the Mount of Transfiguration. What did Jesus mean in Matthew 16:28 when He spoke to Peter, James, and John?

Assuredly I say to you, there are some standing here who shall not taste death till they see the Son of Man coming in His kingdom.

Many believers get confused while interpreting the meaning of certain scriptures because they fail to recognize that while every word of the Bible is divinely inspired of the Holy Spirit, chapter divisions are not!

Chapter divisions were inserted by the hands of mere mortal men centuries ago. The fact is, Matthew 16 and 17 are related in concept, and to fully understand the meaning of Matthew 16:28 we must connect the last verse of Matthew 16 to Matthew 17:1–2.

Now after six days Jesus took Peter, James, and John his brother, led them up on a high mountain by themselves; and He was transfigured before them. His face shone like the sun, and His clothes became as white as the light.

The Lord Jesus Christ was glorified before His death and

resurrection and this is the picture given here. Understand this truth: what happened on the Mount of Transfiguration recorded in Matthew 16 and 17 was an abbreviated portrait of the kingdom of God.

The kingdom of God was reflected by the presence of Moses, who represented the law, and Elijah, who represented the prophets of the Old Testament. They were discussing the forthcoming death, burial, and resurrection of Jesus (Luke 9:30–31 NIV).

Two men, Moses and Elijah, appeared in glorious splendor, talking with Jesus. They spoke about his departure, which he was about to bring to fulfillment at Jerusalem.

Moses and Elijah represented the dead saints of the Old Testament, and Peter, James, and John represented the living saints. The church was not yet in existence; Peter, James, and John would soon represent the body of the New Testament believers, which *is* the church.[4]

The transfiguration of Christ occurred before He died on the cross; the church did not yet exist. If it did not exist, it could not have been raptured.

DECEPTION IN THE CHURCH
Paul writes the following to the believers in Thessalonica:

Now we request you, brethren, with regard to the coming of our Lord Jesus Christ and our gathering together to Him, that you not be quickly shaken from your composure or be disturbed either by a spirit or a message or a letter as if from us, to the effect that the day of the Lord has come. Let no one in any way deceive you, for *it will not come* unless the apostasy comes first, and the man of lawlessness is revealed, the son of destruction, who opposes and exalts himself above every so-called god or object of worship, so that he takes his seat in the temple of God, displaying himself as being God. Do you not remember that while I was still with you, I was telling you these things? (2 Thessalonians 2:1–5 NASB)

The "day of the Lord" in this verse has nothing to do with the church; it has to do with a "day" of God's judgment on the earth that occurs after the rapture—beginning with the Great Tribulation and going through the Millennium.

Apparently someone in the first-century church had fabricated a "letter from us" (meaning Paul, Timothy, or Silas) and was deceiving the Christians in Thessalonica, leading them to believe they were *in* the Great Tribulation. Because of the persecution the church was experiencing at the time, it was a distortion of the truth that was easily believed.

Paul writes his letter to the believers in the church of

Thessalonica that the counterfeit letter and its message were false.[5]

As I have stated before, Joel describes the actual coming of the "day of the Lord":

And I will show wonders in the heavens and in the earth:
Blood and fire and pillars of smoke.
The sun shall be turned into darkness,
And the moon into blood,
Before the coming of the great and awesome day of
the LORD.

(JOEL 2:30–31)

These two verses describe the occurrence of Blood Moons. As you will soon learn, God is speaking to us in the heavens, through the Blood Moons. His message will be on display for the world to see. But to recognize His heavenly announcement, we first need to understand how these Blood Moons relate to the Jewish people and the end times.

The following chapter is biblical evidence of the eternal covenant between God and the Jewish people, which has never been broken and is binding to this day.

It makes no difference what Washington, DC, thinks . . . what Iran wants . . . what Russia demands . . . or what the European Union hopes for—it only matters what God Almighty has declared! He has all power in heaven and on earth!

CHAPTER 7
Land of Promise, Land of Pain

....

Arise, walk in the land through its length and its
width, for I give it to you.

—Genesis 13:17

....

The real estate contract between God Almighty and Abraham, Isaac, and Jacob is recorded repeatedly in the Word of God. The borders and boundaries are clearly stated in the title policy registered in Scripture.

Yet no piece of real estate on planet earth has been more contested than the land of Israel even though God clearly gave it to the Jewish people forever.

There are those who state that the Palestinians have a claim to the land through Ishmael. The Scripture clearly states that God eliminated Ishmael from all consideration to the land of Israel.

> Abraham said to God, "Oh, that Ishmael might live before You!" Then God said, "No, Sarah your wife shall bear you a son, and you shall call his name Isaac; I will establish My covenant with him for an everlasting covenant, and with his descendants after him."
>
> (GENESIS 17:18–19)

Even though God did *not* give the land to Ishmael, He *did* bless him by declaring that he would produce twelve princes that would become a mighty nation (v. 20). Those nations are now known as OPEC. Isaac, the son of covenant, got the land promised to Abraham, and that land is known as Israel today.

Some say that the issue of inheritance between Ishmael and Isaac was only directly referred to in the Old Testament. However, when Paul wrote to the Galatians he used the sons of Hagar and Sarah as an allegory to teach about law and grace. In doing so, he quoted the prophet Isaiah (54:1) and the book of Genesis (21:10) to reiterate the true heir to the land.

> Tell me, you who want to be under the law, are you not aware of what the law says? For it is written that Abraham had two sons, one by the slave woman and the

other by the free woman. His son by the slave woman was born according to the flesh, but his son by the free woman was born as the result of a divine promise.

These things are being taken figuratively: The women represent two covenants. One covenant is from Mount Sinai and bears children who are to be slaves: This is Hagar. Now Hagar stands for Mount Sinai in Arabia and corresponds to the present city of Jerusalem, because she is in slavery with her children. But the Jerusalem that is above is free, and she is our mother. For it is written:

"Be glad, barren woman,
you who never bore a child;
shout for joy and cry aloud,
you who were never in labor;
because more are the children of the desolate woman
than of her who has a husband" [Isaiah 54:1].

Now you, brothers and sisters, like Isaac, are children of promise. At that time the son born according to the flesh persecuted the son born by the power of the Spirit. It is the same now. *But what does Scripture say?* "Get rid of the slave woman and her son, for the slave woman's son *will never share* in the inheritance with the free woman's son" [Genesis 21:10]. Therefore, brothers

and sisters, we are not children of the slave woman,
but of the free woman.

(GALATIANS 4:21–31 NIV)

Paul was as direct as only he can be when he answers the question, "What does Scripture say?" about who owns the "land, leaving no doubt" as to who inherited the Promised Land; it was Isaac not Ishmael.

Why is this important? Because the world is about to explode into World War III over who owns the land of Israel, as Iran races toward the development of a nuclear bomb that will destabilize the world forever. The greatest geopolitical threat to America and the world can be resolved by answering the question: to whom does the land of Israel truly belong? God resolved this controversy centuries ago.

In the following pages, I have given twenty-five Bible references to emphasize God's desire for the Jewish people to exclusively own this land forever.

1. Now the LORD had said to Abram:
"Get out of your country,
From your family
And from your father's house,
To a land that I will show you.
I will make you a great nation;
I will bless you

And make your name great;
And you shall be a blessing.
I will bless those who bless you,
And I will curse him who curses you;
And in you all the families of the earth shall be blessed."

(Genesis 12:1–7)

2. The Lord said to Abram, after Lot had separated from him: "Lift your eyes now and look from the place where you are—northward, southward, eastward and westward; for all the *land which you see I give to you and your descendants forever.*"

(Genesis 13:14–15)

3. Then He said to him, "I am the Lord, who brought you out of Ur of the Chaldeans, *to give you this land to inherit it.*" And [Abram] said, "Lord God, how shall I know that I will inherit it?" So He said to him, "Bring Me a three-year-old heifer, a three-year-old female goat, a three-year-old ram, a turtledove, and a young pigeon." Then he brought all these to Him and cut them in two, down the middle, and placed each piece opposite the other; but he did not cut the birds in two.

(Genesis 15:7–10)

4. And it came to pass, when the sun went down and it was dark, that behold, there appeared a smoking oven and a burning torch that passed between those pieces. On the same day the LORD made a covenant with Abram, saying: *"To your descendants I have given this land*, from the river of Egypt to the great river, the River Euphrates—the Kenites, the Kenezzites, the Kadmonites, the Hittites, the Perizzites, the Rephaim, the Amorites, the Canaanites, the Girgashites, and the Jebusites."

(GENESIS 15:17–21)

5. *Abraham gave all that he had to Isaac.* But Abraham gave gifts to the sons of the concubines which Abraham had; and while he was still living he sent them eastward, away from Isaac his son, to the country of the east.

(GENESIS 25:5–6)

6. There was a famine in the land, besides the first famine that was in the days of Abraham. And Isaac went to Abimelech king of the Philistines, in Gerar [Gaza]. Then the Lord appeared to him and said: "Do not go down to Egypt; live in the land of which I shall tell you. *Dwell in this land, and I will be with you and bless you; for to you and your descendants I give all these*

lands, and I will perform the oath which I swore to Abraham your father. And I will make your descendants multiply as the stars of heaven; I will give to your descendants all these lands; and in your seed all the nations of the earth shall be blessed; because Abraham obeyed My voice and kept My charge, My commandments, My statutes, and My laws." So Isaac dwelt in Gerar [Gaza].

(GENESIS 26:1–6)

7. Now Jacob went out from Beersheba and went toward Haran. So he came to a certain place and stayed there all night, because the sun had set. And he took one of the stones of that place and put it at his head, and he lay down in that place to sleep. Then he dreamed, and behold, a ladder was set up on the earth, and its top reached to heaven; and there the angels of God were ascending and descending on it. And behold, the LORD stood above it and said: "*I am the LORD God of Abraham your father and the God of Isaac; the land on which you lie I will give to you and your descendants.*"

(GENESIS 28:10–13)

8. *I have come down to deliver them* out of the hand of the Egyptians, and *to bring them up from that land to a good and large land*, to a land flowing with milk and

honey, to the place of the Canaanites and the Hittites and the Amorites and the Perizzites and the Hivites and the Jebusites.

(Exodus 3:8)

9. God spoke to Moses and said to him: "I am the Lord. I appeared to Abraham, to Isaac, and to Jacob, as God Almighty, but by My name Lord I was not known to them. *I have also established My covenant with them, to give them the land of Canaan, the land of their pilgrimage, in which they were strangers*."

(Exodus 6:2–4)

10. Therefore say to the children of Israel: "I am the Lord; I will bring you out from under the burdens of the Egyptians, I will rescue you from their bondage, and I will redeem you with an outstretched arm and with great judgments. I will take you as My people, and I will be your God. Then you shall know that I am the Lord your God who brings you out from under the burdens of the Egyptians. And *I will bring you into the land which I swore to give to Abraham, Isaac, and Jacob; and I will give it to you as a heritage*: I am the Lord."

(Exodus 6:6–8)

11. *Then I will remember My covenant with Jacob,* and My covenant *with Isaac* and My covenant *with Abraham* I will remember; I will remember the land.

(LEVITICUS 26:42)

12. Command the children of Israel, and say to them: "When you come into *the land of Canaan, this is the land that shall fall to you as an inheritance*—the land of Canaan to its boundaries."

(NUMBERS 34:2)

13. *See, I have set the land before you; go in and possess the land which the* LORD *swore to your fathers*—to Abraham, Isaac, and Jacob—to give to them and their descendants after them.

(DEUTERONOMY 1:8)

14. Moses my servant is dead. Now therefore, arise, go over this Jordan, you and all this people, *to the land which I am giving to them—the children of Israel.* Every place that the sole of your foot will tread upon I have given you, as I said to Moses. From the wilderness and this Lebanon as far as the great river, the River Euphrates, all the land of the Hittites, and to the Great Sea [Mediterranean Sea] toward the going down of the sun, shall be your territory.

(JOSHUA 1:2–4)

15. . . . and send rain on *Your land which You have given to Your people as an inheritance.*

(1 KINGS 8:36)

16. O seed of Israel His servant,
You children of Jacob, His chosen ones!
He is the LORD our God;
His judgments are in all the earth.
Remember His covenant forever,
The word which He commanded, for a thousand generations,
The covenant which He made with Abraham,
And His oath to Isaac,
And confirmed it to Jacob for a statute,
To Israel for an *everlasting covenant,*
Saying, "To you I will give the land of Canaan
As the allotment of your inheritance."

(1 CHRONICLES 16:13–18)

17. Then hear from heaven and forgive the sin of Your people Israel, and *bring them back to the land which You gave to them and their fathers.*

(2 CHRONICLES 6:25)

18. You gave them bread from heaven for their hunger,
And brought them water out of the rock for their thirst,
And told them to *go in to possess the land*

Which You had sworn to give them.

(NEHEMIAH 9:15)

19. He remembers His covenant forever,

The word which He commanded, for a thousand generations,

The covenant which He made with Abraham,

And His oath to Isaac,

And confirmed it to Jacob for a statute,

To Israel as an everlasting covenant,

Saying, "To you I will give the land of Canaan

As the allotment of your inheritance."

(PSALM 105:8–11)

20. Also your people shall all be righteous;

They shall inherit the land forever,

The branch of My planting,

The work of My hands,

That I may be glorified.

(ISAIAH 60:21)

21. "Behold, the days are coming," says the LORD, "that I will bring back from captivity My people Israel and Judah," says the LORD. "And *I will cause them to return to the land that I gave to their fathers,* and they shall possess it."

(JEREMIAH 30:3)

22. I will take you from among the nations, gather you out of all countries, and *bring you into your own land.*

(EZEKIEL 36:24)

23. *Then I will sow her for Myself in the earth,*
And I will have mercy on her who had not obtained mercy,
Then I will say to those who were not My people,
"You are My people!"
And they shall say, "You are my God!"

(HOSEA 2:23)

24. I will also gather all nations,
And bring them down to the Valley of Jehoshaphat;
And I will enter into judgment with them there
On account of *My people, My heritage Israel,*
Whom they have scattered among the nations;
They have also divided up My land.

(JOEL 3:2)

25. *I will plant them in their land,*
And no longer shall they be pulled up
From the land I have given them,
Says the LORD your God.

(AMOS 9:15)

I have provided these scriptures to establish in your mind how urgently God wants mankind to understand the eternal importance of His covenant of the Land with the Jewish people!

God never breaks covenant! The above body of scriptures proves beyond all reasonable doubt that God gave to the Jewish people a specific piece of real estate that was to be theirs and was forever sealed by a blood covenant. That covenant cannot be rescinded by Russia, Syria, Iran and its radical legions, Hamas, Hezbollah, or even the United Nations and America. God will crush any nation that tries to drive the Jewish people off their sacred soil called Israel (Joel 3:2).

THE DECEIT OF REPLACEMENT THEOLOGY

Some Christians teach that God has broken covenant with the Jewish people. This teaching has come to be known as *Replacement Theology*; some refer to it as *Supersessionism*.

Replacement Theology is a doctrine that presents three false concepts:

1. God is finished with the Jewish people.
2. The New Israel (the Christian church) takes the place of the Jewish people in the economy of God forever.
3. God has broken covenant with the Jewish people and substituted His covenant with the Christian church.

One of the texts typically used as a foundation for Replacement Theology is the parable of the fig tree (Matthew 21:18–22).

These verses are falsely interpreted by Replacement advocates who teach that the fig tree represents the Jewish people, with the emphasis being put on the words of Jesus, "Let no fruit grow on you *ever again*" (Matthew 21:19). But the true message of this parable is the *authority* of the believer, not the state of Israel. In 21:21–22 Jesus said to His disciples, who saw the withered tree:

> Assuredly, I say to you, if you [the believer] have faith and do not doubt, you will not only do what was done to the fig tree, but also if you say to this mountain, "Be removed and be cast into the sea," it will be done. And whatever things you ask in prayer, believing, you will receive.

The central theme of this text is the authority of the believer in all things—even power over nature, not the replacement of the Jewish people.

National Israel was reborn in May 1948 and is today one of the most prosperous nations in the world. It has more patents for new inventions per capita than any nation on earth.[1] Spiritual Israel never ceased to be, and national Israel is flourishing like few nations on the face of the earth!

The second Replacement concept, asserting that the Christian church has replaced the Jewish people, is a complete disregard for Scripture. God made an eternal covenant with Abraham, Isaac, and Jacob and their seed forever that the land of Israel belonged to them by a blood covenant that was eternal.

Why is the ownership of the land of Israel so crucial to our generation? Specifically, there are about 120 million hostile Arabs screaming for the blood of the Jewish people today, and threatening to plunge the Middle East and the world into World War III.

What is the issue? It is the *issue* that has Iran building a nuclear bomb . . . the *issue* that has Hamas and Hezbollah loading long-range missiles to attack Jerusalem . . . the *issue* that is at the heart of the foremost geopolitical crisis of our generation: to whom does the land of Israel belong?

Here is God's position!

God created the heavens and the earth and as the Owner of the heavens and the earth, He chose to make a real estate covenant with Abraham and his descendants decreeing that the land of Israel would belong to the seed of Abraham forever. He sealed the deed with a blood covenant. God is not man that He should lie and He does what He says He will do! (Numbers 23:19).

Those who teach Replacement Theology—which holds that God has broken covenant with the Jewish people and *replaced* them with the church—need to stop and ask themselves a very important question: If God has broken covenant with His own flesh and blood, what confidence do we, as Gentiles, have that He will not break covenant with us?

Paul weighs in on the subject of Replacement Theology with the question recorded in Romans 11:1: "I say then, has God *cast away* His people? Certainly not! For I also am an Israelite, of the seed of Abraham, of the tribe of Benjamin."

Paul's logic is flawless! He is saying, "I am a Jew. If God has cast away the Jewish people, then why is He using me to establish the New Testament church?" Paul repeats his position for those dull of hearing and those slow to catch on:

I say then, have they [the Jewish people] stumbled that they should fall? Certainly not!

(ROMANS 11:11)

The Greek rendering of "certainly not" is the strongest language permitted in the Greek text. Paul is making it very clear that there is no way God has cut off the Jewish people from His blessing, His love, His mercy, or the eternal covenant He made with Abraham, Isaac, and Jacob and the land of Israel.

WHATEVER GOD REMOVES NEVER REAPPEARS

Replacement Theology is based on a bogus premise because whatever God removes never reappears. God removed Sodom and Gomorrah, and it has never been relocated. Some geologists even believe it's at the bottom of the Dead Sea.[2]

Israel is the only nation ever created by a sovereign act of God, which is recorded in Scripture, including its clear boundaries. God created Israel. God defends Israel, for "He who keeps Israel shall neither slumber nor sleep" (Psalm 121:4). God promised to restore Israel from the Diaspora ("scattering") of AD 70.

That promise was fulfilled in May 1948 when the exiles of Israel were gathered from the four corners of the earth and brought back to the land of covenant God gave the Jewish people.

The prophet Amos makes it very clear that when the Jewish people return from exile, they will "never again be uprooted" from their land (9:14–15). Never again . . . means *never again*!

God has not replaced Israel, because as we will see in coming chapters, His heavenly billboard of the Four Blood Moons is directly tied to significant events in the history of the Jewish people. And when Jesus Christ returns to earth as Messiah and King of kings, He is going to identify with the Jewish people.

Jesus introduces Himself in Revelation 5:5 as "The Lion of the tribe of Judah, the Root of David." In His earthly ministry Jesus was a Jewish rabbi, and He will return as "this same Jesus," according to Acts 1:11. The Jewish people have certainly not been cast aside, not now or in the future.

According to Paul's testimony, Jesus is in heaven right now speaking Hebrew.

And when we had all fallen to the ground I heard a voice saying to me in the Hebrew dialect, "Saul, Saul, 'why are you persecuting Me?'"

(ACTS 26:14 NASB)

Do you think He's going to come back in a grey flannel suit looking like an evangelical preacher? Not hardly! He will be wearing a yarmulke underneath His crown and a prayer shawl (tallit) upon His shoulders!

God Almighty has not replaced the Jewish people, because in Revelation 7, He chooses one hundred forty-four thousand Jews to be witnesses for Him during the Tribulation. Why would He use a people He has cast aside?

The first thing Jesus will do in His millennial kingdom is to have the judgment of the nations. The purpose of the judgment of the nations (Matthew 25) is to punish all nations that abused the Jewish people. If God has cast aside the Jews, why would He judge nations for doing what He has been accused of doing by those who present Replacement Theology?

THE STARS AND THE SAND

Immediately following Abraham's willingness to sacrifice Isaac, the Lord said to Abraham:

By Myself I have sworn, says the LORD, because you have done this thing, and have not withheld your son, your only son—blessing I will bless you, and multiplying I will multiply your descendants *as the stars* of the heaven and as *the sand which is on the seashore*; and your descendants shall possess the gate of their enemies.

(GENESIS 22:16–17)

God identified Abraham's descendants *as the stars of the heavens* and *the sands of the seashore*.

The purpose of stars in Scripture:

1. They produce light (Daniel 12:3; Genesis 1:14–15).
2. They rule the darkness of the night (Genesis 1:16–18).
3. They rule in heavenly places (Ephesians 6:12).
4. They are prophetic messengers; part of God's heavenly billboard (Joel 2:30–31; Luke 21:25, 27–28; Acts 2:19–20).

The stars represent Abraham's spiritual seed, which is the church, for Abraham is "the father of us all [all who believe]" (Romans 4:16–17).

The purpose of the church is to be a light in a dark world. The Bible says, "Let your light so shine before men, that they may see your good works and glorify your Father in heaven" (Matthew 5:16).

Jesus said to the church, "You are the light of the world" (Matthew 5:14). The purpose of the kingdom of light is to rule over the kingdom of darkness.

Paul makes that clear in Hebrews 11:12: "Therefore from one man [Abraham] and him as good as dead, were born as many as the stars of the sky in multitude—innumerable as the sand which is by the seashore."

Sand of the sea represents the physical children of Abraham through Isaac, who are the Jewish people. The sand is forever connected to the land so the Jewish people are forever connected to the land of Israel by covenant.

Concerning replacement—the stars never replace sand, and sand never replaces the stars. Each has its own sovereign purpose from God to exist. Israel and the church are unique. The church never replaces Israel, and Israel never replaces the church.

Replacement Theology is intellectually and scripturally dishonest. I believe Replacement Theology is religious anti-Semitism; it is one of the most dangerous forms of deception in the church today.

CHAPTER 8
Wars and Rumors of Wars

You will hear of wars and rumors of wars, but see to
it that you are not alarmed. Such things must happen,
but the end is still to come. Nation will rise against
nation, and kingdom against kingdom.

—MATTHEW 24:6–7 NIV1984

As a student of history, allow me to plant a seed of thought in
your mind.

Begin with the basic concept that God is sovereign. He
controls the lives of men, the destiny of nations, and all events
that happen in the universe.

Next, consider that God, as Creator and Owner of planet

earth, made a real estate covenant with Abraham, Isaac, and Jacob, and their seed that the land of Israel, with boundaries established in the Bible, belongs to the Jewish people forever (Genesis 15:18–21; 17:7–8).

Remember this very important fact; the Jewish people do not *occupy* the land; they *own* the land!

Continue the logic that a sovereign God has made a pledge to the Jewish people that "He that keepeth Israel shall neither slumber nor sleep" (Psalm 121:4 KJV). *Keepeth* is a military term meaning "to defend and protect." The major battles in the Bible had to do with God defending the Jewish people, "the apple of His eye" (Zechariah 2:8). Any nation or group of nations that tried to eliminate Israel was wiped out by the God of Abraham, Isaac, and Jacob.

The enemies of the children of Israel at the Battle of Jericho, and the five armies at the Battle of Five Kings (Joshua 10) who tried to annihilate Israel as they journeyed from Egypt to the Promised Land, were stoned to death by God Himself when they attacked Israel. The Bible records the battle graphically:

> And it happened, as they fled before Israel . . . that the
> LORD cast down large hailstones from heaven on them
> . . . and they [five armies] died. There were more who
> died from the hailstones than the children of Israel
> killed with the sword.
>
> (JOSHUA 10:11)

David, the shepherd boy, killed Goliath with the help of the Lord and the fling of his sling shot. In doing so, he saved Israel from becoming enslaved by the Philistines. This one act of bravery liberated Israel to produce the prophets who would pen the Holy Scriptures for the world to read. It liberated Israel to bring forth King David and ultimately King David's great-great grandson—Jesus of Nazareth, who liberated the world from the kingdom of darkness.

When Haman plotted to kill the Jews in Persia [modern Iran], he and his sons were hung on the gallows they built to hang the Jews. God was watching! Most of the Jews in the world at this point in history lived in Persia. For them to have been annihilated would have hindered the purposes of God. God saw to it that the architect of the Old Testament Holocaust hanged on the very gallows he built for the Jews.

Jesus told us that before His second coming, we "will hear of wars and rumors of wars" and that "nation will rise against nation, and kingdom against kingdom" (Matthew 24:6–7 NIV1984). I believe that "nation will rise against nation" describes all major physical wars on earth from the time of Christ until today, including the wars against Israel.

The point is this: God Almighty created the Jewish State and has sworn to defend it. Anyone—politicians from Haman to Hitler, military giants from Goliath to Iran, or any tormentor from Pharaoh to Putin—that presents an existential threat to Israel will utterly be destroyed by the hand of the Lord.

God is jealous, and the LORD avenges;
The LORD avenges and is furious.
The LORD will take vengeance on His adversaries,
And He reserves wrath for His enemies.

(NAHUM 1:2)

WORLD WAR I

As we study the history of the Jewish people related to biblical prophecy, let us consider the impact of World War I on the State of Israel.

In World War I, the British were cut off from their source to make cordite gunpowder. First Lord of the Admiralty Winston Churchill went to Chaim Weizmann, a Jewish chemist, and asked him if he could find a way to make several tons of synthetic gunpowder. Without it bullets couldn't be fired, artillery was useless, and cannons on ships were mere ornaments. The outcome of the war was at stake.

Weizmann and his associates discovered how to make this massive amount of synthetic gunpowder within weeks. This Jewish inventor played a major role in the victory of WWI over Germany.

After the war, Lord Balfour asked Chaim Weizmann what England could do to honor him. Weizmann asked that his people (the Jews) be given a homeland.

Lord Balfour created a historic document known to this

day as the Balfour Declaration, giving the Jewish people what God had already guaranteed in the book of Genesis—a homeland.

Though the Balfour Declaration went through several drafts, the final version was issued on November 2, 1917, in a letter from Balfour to Lord Rothschild, president of the British Zionist Federation.

The Zionists of the world continued to return to the Land of Promise. God's all-seeing eye was watching over the seed of Abraham as He was regathering the exiles from the nations of the world.[1]

WORLD WAR II

In His discourse on the Mount of Olives, Jesus described the horror of future events, saying, "Unless those days were shortened, no flesh would be saved; but for the elect's sake [the Jewish people] those days will be shortened" (Matthew 24:22). This verse clearly points to the coming Holocaust of the Jews, because the references in the Olivet Discourse to "the elect" refer to the Jewish people—not the church.

Adolf Hitler was a demonized, anti-Semitic monster who came to power by virtue of the Treaty of Versailles, which mandated that Germany pay to America and England all expenses for World War I. It was an astronomical cost.

In an effort to comply to this treaty Germany bankrupted itself by monetizing the debt, a method of financing national debt through printing new money, which inflates the currency until it has absolutely no value due to its huge supply. America is doing exactly this right now, as we race toward a twenty-trillion-dollar national debt.

Hitler came to power promising the German people that he would not pay the debt to America and England for World War I. He vowed instead to invest in the German people by rebuilding the national highway infrastructure, which became known as the Autobahn, creating a car, which became the Volkswagen (people's car), and reinstating their military. The people were thrilled; Hitler did not shoot his way to power; he was voted in by a well-educated and highly sophisticated German society.[2]

Hitler hated the Jewish people just as radical Islamists hate the Jewish people. Before coming to power Hitler wrote *Mein Kampf*, which means "My Struggle." It is no coincidence that the word *jihad* also means "my struggle." Both Hitler's struggle and the struggle of radical Islam was and is with the Jewish people. Both declared war and destruction against the seed of Abraham.

Hitler made it clear in *Mein Kampf* that he intended to kill the Jewish people. The world simply did not believe he would do it. The birth of the "Final Solution" and the death of six million Jews is living proof he meant every word.

The anti-Semitic spirit of Haman and Hitler lives on.

Mahmoud Ahmadinejad, former president of Iran, repeatedly ranted for the whole world to hear that his mission was to wipe Israel off the face of the map. America's leaders chose not to take him seriously!

Iran has recently elected a new leader, and Israel Prime Minister Benjamin Netanyahu, knowing the mindset of Israel's enemies, said, "We do not delude ourselves and must not be caught up in wishful thinking and be tempted to relax the pressure on Iran to halt its nuclear program."

Mark Dubowitz, executive director of the Foundation for Defense of Democracies, was quoted as saying,

> Iran's new president will negotiate to play for time in order to reach an industrial-size nuclear weapons capacity and a nuclear breakout which will allow Iran, without detection, to produce enough weapons-grade uranium or separated plutonium for one or more bombs. The election of [Hassan] Rowhani, a master of nuclear deceit, doesn't get us any closer to stopping Iran's nuclear drive.[3]

History does repeat itself; we are living 1938 all over again! This time let us not be silent in the face of evil.

World War II was brought to an early close through the scientific genius of Albert Einstein, who was instrumental in developing the atomic bomb. America's military experts predicted that at least seven hundred and fifty thousand American lives were saved that would have otherwise been lost in a land invasion of Japan.[4]

How did that affect Israel? The shortening of WWII ended the Holocaust. One-third of European Jewry had been "wiped out"—Hitler's goal was total extermination.

General Dwight D. Eisenhower ordered the global media to film the unspeakable hell of the Holocaust. General Eisenhower feared there would come a day when there would be "Holocaust deniers" who would declare it never happened.[5]

Today, Iran's radical Islamic leaders, who have promised to wipe the Jews off the face of the map, are indeed Holocaust deniers.[6] Sadly, their venom is gathering international support.

From the tears and tragedy of World War II came the rebirth of the State of Israel in May 1948. Ezekiel prophesied concerning God's promise to bring the exiles home to Israel:

> For indeed I am for you. . . . I will multiply men upon you, all the house of Israel, all of it; and the cities shall be inhabited and the ruins rebuilt. . . . For I will take you from among the nations, gather you out of all countries, and bring you into your own land. . . . Then you shall dwell in the land that I gave to your fathers; you shall be My people, and I will be your God.
>
> (EZEKIEL 36:9–10, 24, 28)

WORLD WAR III

World War III is coming!

We can see the storm gathering in the Middle East and, again, Israel is the key. Russia, Iran, Germany, Turkey, Libya, and the Arab Spring nations have surrounded Israel, the island of freedom and democracy, in an ocean of terror and tyranny.

God is watching!

The final drama is unfolding before our eyes as you read it on the front pages of your newspaper and watch it on the national news almost every night.

The second rider of the Apocalypse will ride in on a red horse, bringing war and bloodshed. God will destroy the enemies of Israel in the most supernatural display of His power ever seen since He crushed Pharaoh and his army in the Red Sea. God will protect Israel—and the course of history will be changed forever.

KINGDOM SHALL RISE AGAINST KINGDOM

I believe Jesus' prophecy that kingdom shall rise against kingdom (Matthew 24:7) is a description of the kingdom of light versus the kingdom of darkness. It's the final battle between the Author of truth and the father of lies, the battle of good versus evil.

The battle against good and evil is raging now! Look at your television programming and movie advertisements presenting the occult . . . the demonic . . . the satanic . . . the practice of witchcraft and sorcery in popular books . . . the open hostility toward Christianity and the revival of anti-Semitism. The fight is on for the hearts and minds of our children in ours homes, our schools, our universities, and our society.

Our children are being programmed to be slaves of the socialist state; there will come a time when they will believe the government over the Word of God.

Recently, a forty-seven-year-old recording of one of America's foremost radio personalities, Paul Harvey, was released. With his trademark insight, Paul Harvey described the battle of the kingdom of light and the kingdom of darkness with chilling accuracy:

> If I were the devil . . . If I were the Prince of Darkness, I'd want to engulf the whole world in darkness. . . . So I'd set about however necessary to take over the United States.
>
> I'd subvert the churches first—I'd begin with a campaign of whispers. With the wisdom of a serpent, I would whisper to you as I whispered to Eve: "Do as you please." To the young, I would whisper that "The Bible is a myth." I would convince them that man created God instead of the other way around. I would confide that what's bad is good, and what's good is "square." And the old, I would teach to pray, after me,

"Our Father, which art in Washington . . ." In other words, if I were the devil I'd just keep right on doing what he's doing.[7]

If America is to survive, there must be a time of national repentance for our sins and a return to the eternal truths of the Word of God. Selah!

CHAPTER 9
Famine, Earthquakes, and Anarchy

....

When he opened the third seal, I heard the third

living creature say, "Come and see."

So I looked, and behold, a black horse, and he

who sat on it had a pair of scales in his hand.

And I heard a voice in the midst of the four living

creatures saying, "A quart of wheat for a denarius,

and three quarts of barley for a denarius;

and do not harm the oil and the wine."

—Revelation 6:5–6

....

The vision John had while on the isle of Patmos describes the
third rider of the Apocalypse. John sees a rider on a black

horse, who is carrying a pair of scales allowing him to exactly weigh the wheat and barley he is selling for a denarius. John the Revelator is painting a portrait of a global famine.

A denarius was the equivalent of one day's earnings for the average working man (Matthew 20:2). John is saying that a typical family will pay a full day's wage for a quart of wheat. How long would a quart of wheat feed *your* family?

After you've spent your entire day's salary for one day's food ration, what must you do to pay for your housing and upkeep, for your clothing and medical expenses, or fuel— which *alone* will be worth its weight in gold?

During this time of famine the church of Jesus Christ will be in heaven sitting at the marriage supper of the Lamb as honored guests of the Master. But what about those who are left behind? What will they experience?

Americans are isolated from the famines the world is already experiencing. The World Hunger Organization reported that in 1996 up to 3.5 million people were the victims of famine in North Korea. In a six year span, between 1998 to 2004, the Democratic Republic of Congo reported the deaths of 3.8 million people due to famine.[1]

The American Red Cross, in their annual survey, estimated 17.2 million American households (1 out of 7) were "food insecure."[2]

After a time of war (red horse) there is always a time of shortage; this time will be no different. The world, *including*

America, is inching toward a time when we will no longer be able to produce the food it takes to feed our people.

THE DEMISE OF THE FAMILY FARM

The family farm in America is being systematically wiped out of existence. "According to the U.S. Department of Agriculture, the number of farms in the United States has fallen from 6.8 million in 1935 to only about two million today."[3]

Farming in America is now dominated by major oil companies and agribusiness conglomerates, making it impossible for the average farmer to compete. "According to Farm Aid, every week approximately 330 farmers leave their land for good. . . . A very large percentage of family farmers are in their fifties, sixties or seventies . . . only 6 percent of all farmers are under the age of thirty-five."[4] There is no "Joshua's Generation" to carry on the American family farm.

Not only are major conglomerates driving the average farmer out of business . . . not only is farmland becoming a prime target for real estate investors . . . not only is the exponential trend of migration from rural to urban life a major factor partly because the next generation views farm life as nothing more than a twelve-hour-a-day sweat shop with little or no profit. But America now has wealthy foreign investors like China[5] and Japan who already hold most of the US debt in the form of federal notes (treasury securities), purchasing large amounts of American farmland. As this book goes to print, China is trying to purchase the largest pork production enterprise in America. All the pork produced in this plant will go directly to China.

In addition, the IRS *death tax,* which can exceed 50 percent of a farm's total value, is lurking in the wings hastening the inevitable demise of the American farm. For example, if your father owns a farm valued at one million dollars at the time of his death, the IRS will be on your doorstep demanding as much as 50 percent of the value of your deceased father's property. You will be forced to sell the farm to raise the $500,000 to pay the IRS or lose your land.[6]

This ever-worsening crisis of foreign-owned American farmland will eventually lead to massive food shortages. America is slowly selling the source of our food (our land) due to the indifference of the next generation or due to the burden of paying massive death taxes. The famine is coming. It's just a matter of time.

THERE WILL BE PESTILENCES

I was twelve years old when my grandfather, John Christopher Hagee, passed away. I can only remember seeing my grandfather twice in my lifetime. The first time was in 1948 at a Thanksgiving family reunion, and the second time was at his gravesite in a small town in Oklahoma in the summer of 1952.

While my father, his five surviving brothers, and Grandmother Hagee were hugging each other and saying their goodbyes after the burial, I started wandering through the small country cemetery. Almost immediately I noticed that many of the tombstones of both the elderly and the young cited their date of death as being in 1917.

As I rejoined my father, who was leaving the cemetery, I asked him, "What happened here in 1917?"

He replied, "In 1917 the swine flu swept through our town, and half of this town died in just a few months. I saw horse-drawn hearses carrying two bodies in one casket—a mother holding her baby, both dead with influenza."

"Why didn't these people get a shot?" I asked.

"There was no shot to get—no medicine would touch it. The strong lived and the weak died."

Almost one hundred years have passed since that deadly flu epidemic, and the finest scientific minds in the world warn us that there are viruses that have mutated and are immune to any vaccine that we have created.

Nothing can stop a plague once it starts. It will be just as my father described with the epidemic of 1917—the strong will survive, and the weak will die.

Global scientists are warning the world of a potential pandemic flu outbreak, which usually strikes three to four times a century. Pandemic flu is a strain of flu virus that is capable of spreading rapidly from person to person worldwide. Because we now have metropolises with millions of people living in close proximity, the rate of infection can spread like a prairie fire driven by a fierce wind.

Just a few weeks ago, I was talking across the fence to my neighbor while working on my ranch. He served as a US congressman and now works in Washington, DC, studying the potential of a pandemic bird flu outbreak in America and around the world. My neighbor, who is not an alarmist but a well-reasoned man of outstanding intellect, made a statement that shocked me. He told me without hesitation, "Pastor, it's not a matter of *if*; it's only a matter of *when* we will have a major pandemic bird flu outbreak in America. When it *does* happen, gather all your family on your ranch and isolate yourselves for several months. That will be the price of survival."

I shook my head as I said my good-byes and walked off toward my truck with Jesus' words ringing in my ears: "There will be . . . pestilences" (Matthew 24:7).

When I got home I picked up the April 16–17, 2013, weekend edition of the *Wall Street Journal* and saw a picture of the Chinese killing chickens because of their deep concerns about a new avian flu strain. The CDC is concerned that this deadly bird flu virus could begin to spread from bird to human and then from human to human at any moment.

An outbreak of the H7N3 bird flu virus in western Mexico in 2012 led to the slaughter of more than 22 million hens, causing price increases in chicken and egg products.[7]

America is not immune to pestilence. A new strain of the H3N2 virus is spreading across the United States at a record-breaking speed. According to the Department of Health, the state of Missouri alone reported a nearly 2,000 percent increase in positive flu tests. The Center of Disease Control and Prevention had reports of this virus in forty-one states.[8]

In spite of our medical sophistication, there will be global pestilence.

THERE WILL BE EARTHQUAKES

God uses earthquakes to get the attention of those who are spiritually hard of hearing. God is saying, if you can't see the signs in the heavens, if you refuse to recognize the obvious signs of prophecy fulfilled, let me shake the ground under your feet; let cities be swallowed, mountains leveled, and islands of the sea disappear.

God used an earthquake in the original "Jailhouse Rock." The apostle Paul and Silas were thrown into prison for preaching the gospel. Rather than pout and whine over their persecution, they decided to sing praises to God in the midnight hour.

God shook the foundations of the earth with a "violent earthquake" to bring down prison walls and allow Paul and Silas to make a convert out of their jailer (Acts 16:25–28).

God used an earthquake on resurrection morning as the angel of God "rolled back the stone from the door [of the tomb], and sat on it" (Matthew 28:2). The stone was not removed to let Christ out but to let us in; the greatest news the world has ever heard came out of the graveyard—He lives!

God promises that all nations who battle against Jerusalem

"will be punished by the LORD of hosts with thunder and earthquake and great noise" (Isaiah 29:6).

God forewarns planet earth that the greatest earthquake in human history is coming! John the Revelator describes it with these words:

> There was a great earthquake, such a mighty and great earthquake as had not occurred since men were on the earth.... And the cities of the nations fell.... Then every island fled away, and the mountains were not found.
>
> (REVELATION 16:18–20)

Can you imagine an earthquake so globally severe that the Rocky Mountains, Mount Everest, and Kilimanjaro are shaken until they become pebbles leveled to the ground? Can you visualize planet earth's geography being transformed by an earthquake so great that major islands of the sea like Hawaii, the Philippines, the Solomon Islands, and Great Britain will fall below sea level?

Most Americans are aware of the San Andreas Fault on the West Coast; one strong earthquake near this crevice and millions will experience massive and instant destruction. Can you visualize San Francisco falling into the Pacific Ocean with cities from San Diego to Sacramento ablaze from ruptured gas lines . . . destroyed freeways making the assistance of first responders impossible . . . countless thousands trapped in the rubble of collapsed high-rise apartments and office buildings? That's only a glimpse of the immense destruction of a major earthquake that America's finest geologists confirm as "the Big One is coming."

Few are aware that the Army Corps of Engineers has identified a major fault running the full length of the Mississippi River from New Orleans to Canada. Experts are stating that one major earthquake could split America in half.[9]

The United States Geological Survey reports that global occurrences of earthquakes from 2008 through 2010 totaled 107,135 with 25,449 happening in America alone.

How great is our God? Far greater than the mind of man can imagine, and far greater than anything we've seen in the history of the world! He is crying out to us—the *Big One is coming*!

THE UNITED STATES OF ANARCHY

Jesus told His disciples that before He returns, lawlessness will abound (Matthew 24:12). We hear the words of the Jewish Rabbi speaking to His generation—words that could dominate the headlines of every media outlet in America tomorrow: "Anarchy in America." Jesus painted the portrait of our nation in three words: "Lawlessness will abound" (Matthew 24:12).

The Bible identifies the Antichrist as "the lawless one," and his claim to power and to deity is proved by signs produced through satanic power. He is received as a god on earth and as a ruler because of the blindness of the people who will follow him.

And then the lawless one will be revealed, whom the Lord Jesus will overthrow with the breath of his mouth and destroy by the splendor of his coming. The coming of the lawless one will be in accordance with how Satan works. He will use all sorts of displays of power through signs and wonders that serve the lie, and all the ways that wickedness deceives those who are perishing. They perish because they refused to love the truth and so be saved. For this reason God sends them a powerful delusion so that they will believe the lie.

(2 THESSALONIANS 2:8–11)

The Bible says the "spirit of the Antichrist" (1 John 4:3) is alive in the world today. Certainly we see the spirit of rebellion exploding in America. *Anarchy* is defined by Merriam-Webster as "a state of lawlessness or political disorder due to the absence of governmental authority."

The last verse in the book of Judges records, "In those days there was no king in Israel [no national leadership]; everyone did what was right in his own eyes" (21:25).

When authority goes out, anarchy comes in.

America has a lack of leadership within our government, and we are seeing anarchy on a national level never seen in our history.

Not long ago, protesters rioted in the streets of Wisconsin as unions fought for control of the government.[10] The Occupy

Wall Street mobs of Union Square in New York were the clear portrait of lawlessness in America. For example, "according to a memo written by the FBI's New York field office in August 2011, bureau personnel met with officials from the New York Stock Exchange to discuss 'the planned Anarchist protest titled "Occupy Wall Street,"' scheduled for September 17, 2011."[11]

The protest appeared on anarchist websites and social network pages on the Internet, the memo said. "Numerous incidents have occurred in the past which show attempts by Anarchist groups to disrupt, influence, and/or shut down normal business operations of financial districts."[12]

The world is upside down! Right and wrong are no longer absolute but relative to man's personal opinion. Every man is doing that which is right in his own eyes. "If I think it's right, that makes it right." America has contextual morality and situational ethics. "If you don't like the law, break it; if it makes you feel good . . . do it!" As a result, we have civil chaos.

Daily newscasts show angry mobs holding protest signs and screaming obscenities, demanding special entitlements. America has become a nation of polarizing groups, each with their own agenda and having no regard for the well-being of our country as a whole.

University students protest so violently that speakers with different opinions are driven from the podium and denied their basic right to freedom of speech while administrators stand by and surrender to the mob. When television cameras arrive, the mob grows bigger and more violent. The police are called in to do what the parents of these students refused to do ten years earlier.

There is little discipline in government, in school, in the home, or in most individuals. The rebellion against authority is also alive in the apostate church that has thrown discipline overboard and no longer mentions the necessity of submitting to spiritual and civil leadership.

The alternative to discipline is mayhem where the nation has become an asylum, and the inmates are in charge.

AMERICA'S SPIRITUAL AND MORAL COLLAPSE

America has become so feeble, fearful, permissive, and promiscuous. The forces of evil are taking advantage of our spiritual decline and moral weakness by spreading havoc across our nation.

Thanks to a skewed court system, the offender gets more sympathy than the victim of his crime. Police officers are put on trial for doing their duty against a criminal with a rap sheet that reaches to the floor. Who's the one who broke the law— the criminal or the policeman? Police officers are investigated while criminals write books that make them rich, famous, and features them on television talk shows.

The vicious crime wave in America today is not only wicked but demonic. When young men charge into schools and theaters with assault rifles and thousands of rounds of ammunition to slaughter innocent men, women, and children at will, it's evil and it's demonic! These are no longer crimes, these are the hideous acts of heartless executioners.

There is no king in Israel (America or the world), and every man is doing that which is right in his own eyes. However men may justify it . . . and by whatever name they call it . . . it's anarchy!

Recently, a student attending Florida Atlantic University was told by his instructor, Deandre Poole, to write the name of Jesus on a piece of paper, drop it on the ground, and stomp on it. When the student refused, academic charges were brought against him. A hold was placed on his academic records until a final decision was reached. His faith was under fire! Fox News exposed the story and they obtained a synopsis of the lesson taught by the instructor. When the story became public, Florida Atlantic University issued an apology.[13]

I wonder if the instructor would dare order one of his students to write the name of Muhammad on a piece of paper and stomp on it. Never! The outrage would get him fired, as a mob of irate campus protestors would demand an immediate resignation and complete apology. But in America, attacking Christians has become an art form. The spirit of anarchy rules our nation.

In our spiritual and moral collapse we have forgotten that the definition of marriage is between a man and a woman. We have forgotten that life begins at conception and to destroy life in the womb of a mother is murder in the courts of heaven.

We will face God in the judgment for the death of the unborn in our nation.

We have forgotten that there is a difference between a boy and a girl. "From the city of Fountain, Colorado, comes news of liberal parents who believe their little boy is actually a little girl on the 'inside.'" The parents are insisting that their six-year-old son be allowed to attend classes dressed as a girl and that he be allowed to use the girl's bathroom.[14]

When the school told the parents they would not permit their son to use the girl's bathroom, the parents, with the help of the Transgender Legal Defense and Education Fund, filed a discrimination complaint with the Colorado Civil Rights Division.[15]

America is going in the wrong direction! Wake up, America! Remember what the Word of God says!

Blessed is the nation whose God is the LORD. (PSALM 33:12)

The wicked shall be turned into hell,
And all the nations that forget God. (PSALM 9:17)

Righteousness exalts a nation,
But sin is a reproach to any people. (PROVERBS 14:34)

After describing the lawlessness of the land, Jesus continued His Prophecy Conference with the Twelve by presenting the concept of the *gospel of the kingdom.*

CHAPTER 10
The Gospel of the Kingdom

This gospel of the kingdom will be preached
in all the world as a witness to all the nations,
and then the end will come.

—MATTHEW 24:14

Following the rapture of the church, the Antichrist will be in total control of the earth. He will become the persecutor of those who refuse to receive his mark (Revelation 13:7). Many will die a martyr's death. For this reason Jesus said, "He who endures to the end shall be saved" (Matthew 24:13).

The *gospel of the kingdom* was preached by John the Baptist: "In those days John the Baptist came, preaching in the wilderness of Judea and saying, 'Repent, for the kingdom of heaven is at hand'" (Matthew 3:1–2).

Jesus preached the message of repentance in Matthew 4:17: "From that time on Jesus began to preach, 'Repent, for the kingdom of heaven is at hand.'" Jesus also sent His disciples out with the same message (Matthew 10).

During the reign of the Antichrist, the *gospel of the kingdom* will be preached all over the world. It will be preached by the one hundred forty-four thousand from the twelve tribes of Israel who will be sealed on their foreheads to protect them from the power of the Antichrist who desires to destroy them (Revelation 7:3–4).

God will also send His angels to preach the *gospel of the kingdom* to the nations of the world (Revelation 14:6–7). In addition, God will send Elijah to the Jewish people to tell them, "Messiah is coming!" The last message given to the Jewish people in the Old Testament was to look for the Prophet Elijah:

Behold I will send you Elijah the prophet
Before the coming of the great and dreadful day of the LORD.

(MALACHI 4:5)

For centuries, at every Passover celebration, at a specific point in the meal, Jewish people open the door of their homes for Elijah to enter and be seated at a place at the table reserved exclusively for him.

During the tribulation, Israel will sign a seven-year peace treaty with the Antichrist, which will guarantee their national security from all the hostile nations that now surround them. In my opinion, based on the historical precedent established by Hadrian in AD 135, the Jewish people will also be granted permission by the Antichrist to rebuild the Third Temple on the Temple Mount. Later, the Antichrist will break that treaty and Elijah and Enoch will appear to the Jewish people. These two witnesses will preach the *gospel of the kingdom* with shocking supernatural power. The Bible says:

> If anyone wants to harm them, fire proceeds from their mouth and devours their enemies. . . . These have power to shut heaven, so that no rain falls . . . and they have power over waters to turn them to blood.
>
> (REVELATION 11:5–6)

As a result of the preaching of the gospel of the kingdom, many will come to faith in Christ during the tribulation. In the process of time Paul declares that all Israel will be saved just as he was—by divine revelation when the scales that judicially blinded him to the recognition of Jesus Christ fell from his eyes (Romans 11:25).

The impact of the angels flying through the heavens preaching the gospel of the kingdom and of the two witnesses, will produce a harvest of souls: "a great multitude which no one could number, of all nations, tribes, peoples, and tongues" (Revelation 7:9). The multitudes will have "washed their robes and made them white in the blood of the Lamb" (v. 14).

Until the time of the Rapture, the church is to preach the *gospel of salvation*. It is the message of the first coming of Christ. It speaks of Christ's virgin birth, His life, death, and resurrection. The preaching of the gospel of salvation produces our redemption by grace through faith in Christ, which promises eternal life.

> And you also were included in Christ when you heard
> the message of truth, the *gospel of your salvation*.
> When you believed, you were marked in him with a
> seal, the promised Holy Spirit.
>
> (EPHESIANS 1:13 NIV)

Jesus now reminds his disciples of the coming perilous times referred to by the prophet Daniel as the "abomination of desolation."

THE ABOMINATION OF ANTIOCHUS EPIPHANES

> "Therefore when you see the 'abomination of desola-
> tion,' spoken of by Daniel the prophet, standing in the
> holy place" (whoever reads, let him understand).
>
> (MATTHEW 24:15)

What is the "abomination of desolation"? The abomination of desolation is the desecration of the Temple in Jerusalem and the termination of blood sacrifices for the atonement of sin.

Daniel (7–6 BC) prophesied about the vicious Greek king Antiochus Epiphanes, saying, "Forces from him will arise, desecrate the sanctuary fortress and do away with the regular sacrifice. And they will set up the abomination of desolation" (Daniel 11:31 NASB).

Antiochus Epiphanes ruled the Jews from 175 to 164 BC killing over one hundred thousand during his reign. Epiphanes hated the Jewish people, and in his desire to defile the Temple, he offered a sow on the altar, which, according to the Law of Moses, was an unclean animal making the Temple unclean—and an abomination for the Jewish people (Leviticus 11:7). In addition to offering the sow on the altar, Antiochus set up a statue of the Greek god Jupiter to be worshiped in the Temple of the Lord.

Daniel is prophesying of the "abomination" of Epiphanes. Jesus, in Matthew 24, is referring to the future abomination that will be caused by the Antichrist saying that *he* will be *like* Epiphanes. While Epiphanes placed a Greek idol in the Temple, the Antichrist will set up an image of *himself* for all to worship.

The book of Revelation makes a clear reference to this image:

If anyone worships the beast *and his image,* and receives his mark on his forehead or on his hand, he
himself shall also drink of the wine of the wrath of
God, which is poured out full strength into the cup of
His indignation. He shall be tormented with fire and
brimstone in the presence of the holy angels and in the
presence of the Lamb. And the smoke of their torment
ascends forever and ever; and they have no rest day or
night, who worship the beast and *his image*, and whoever receives the mark of his name.

(REVELATION 14:9–11)

THE ABOMINATION OF GENERAL TITUS

In AD 70, the Roman General Titus was sent to Jerusalem
to crush Jewish resistance against the Roman Empire. Titus
placed on the entrance to the Temple a Roman eagle—an unclean animal according to Jewish law—which was an abomination to the Jewish people (Leviticus 11:13). Roman standards representing their idols were placed in the Temple for all
to worship. This was the "abomination of desecration."

Jerusalem was viciously destroyed, the Temple leveled,
and the Jewish people were banished from their beloved capital. The Roman army built a garrison on the ruins of the city.
Meanwhile, in the city of Rome, the victory over Jerusalem
was celebrated by the construction of the massive Arch of

Titus near the entrance to the Roman Coliseum. I have been there to see this tribute to Titus, who was responsible for the death of hundreds of thousands of Jews.

Over the top of the Arch of Titus is depicted a great military parade of triumphant Roman soldiers carrying away the Temple treasures from Jerusalem, and herding seventy thousand Jewish captives toward Rome. Those Jewish captives were forced to build the Roman Coliseum, where thousands of Christians were later fed to lions and slaughtered for their testimony of faith in Christ. Three words made them an enemy of the state and cost them their lives: "Jesus is Lord!"

In AD 107 the Emperor Trajan came to Antioch and forced the Christians to choose between the Pagan Roman gods and death. Ignatius refused and the emperor condemned him to death by being torn to pieces by wild beasts at Rome— "damnatio ad bestia." Ignatius travelled to Rome, guarded by soldiers, and showed no fear of being devoured by lions in the Roman Colosseum.[1]

The Abomination of Emperor Hadrian

An even greater demonic Roman leader, Hadrian, walked onto the stage of history in AD 117 as emperor of Rome. Hadrian promised the remnant of Jewish people who remained in the city that he would restore Jerusalem and rebuild the

Temple. The Jewish people were jubilant and filled with hope.

In AD 130, Hadrian broke his promise to the Jewish people. Jerusalem would be rebuilt—but as a Roman city named Aelia Capitolina. *Aelia* reflected the second name of Hadrian, which indicated an act of imperial worship. *Capitolina* was a reminder that the city was dedicated to the worship of the Roman gods. At the heart of the paganized city, a temple to Jupiter (Satan) was erected on Mount Zion, desecrating the site of the Holy Temple. This was an abomination of desolation.[2]

Hadrian followed in the footsteps of Antiochus Epiphanes by tormenting the Jewish people. Hadrian outlawed circumcision, the observance of the Sabbath, and prayers in the synagogue in an effort to assimilate the Jews into the Roman Empire.[3]

In his rage against the Jews, Hadrian made an attempt to obliterate their name and existence from the pages of world history. He decreed that all the maps in the Roman Empire would no longer read *Judea* but would read *Palestine* after the name of the ancient enemies of Israel (Philistines). Goliath of Gath was a Philistine.[4]

Historically there has never been an autonomous group of people called Palestinians. Only with the coming of Yasser Arafat in 1959 and his terrorist organization (PLO) did the word *Palestinians* become a distinctive word to describe a specific group of people.

The next cruel dictator to copy the pattern of Hadrian will be the Antichrist, described by the prophet Daniel and referred to by Jesus during His Prophecy Conference.

THE ABOMINATION OF THE ANTICHRIST

Daniel 7:8 refers to the Antichrist when he speaks of "another horn, a little one." In prophetic scripture a "horn" represents a king of an existing or coming empire. This prophecy introduces us to a figure (the Antichrist) who will be elevated to a position of authority over ten nations that arise out of the original Roman Empire.

The one whom John called "the beast" will come to power, not by military conquest but by the request of the people (Revelation 17:13). He will eventually become the leader of the New World Order!

He will appear on the world scene in the "latter time" of Israel's history (Daniel 8:23). He is a Gentile, because he arises from the sea (Revelation 13:1), which represents the nations of the world (Revelation 17:15).

The Antichrist will come from the Roman Empire since he is a ruler of the people who destroyed Jerusalem (Daniel 9:26). He will be a political leader of a world government with seven heads and ten horns (Revelation 13:1). This means that when he comes to power, there will be, for a short time, a New World Order that has ten leaders. The Antichrist will conquer three of those leaders, and he will wear their crowns. Again, he is emulating Jesus Christ, who is King of all kings and Lord of all lords.

The coming Antichrist will be ultimate "abomination of desolation" because he will introduce himself as god (Daniel 11:36–37; Revelation 13:5) and demand that the world worship him. He will set up his image in Jerusalem and present himself as the savior of the world.

This "little horn," this son of perdition—the chief son of Satan—will be anointed to receive demonic power from Satan himself (Ezekiel 28:9–12; Revelation 13:4). He is driven by the demonic spirit of pride given to him directly by the prince of darkness. He will cause deceit to prosper (Daniel 8:25) and be exceedingly arrogant. Daniel states, "He shall magnify himself in his heart, and by peace shall destroy many" (8:25 KJV), which means the Antichrist will make peace treaties he never intends to keep, especially with Israel.

He will blaspheme God, as John the Revelator states: "He opened his mouth in blasphemy against God" (Revelation 13:6). He will force everyone on planet earth to take his mark, and without that mark you cannot buy or sell (vv. 16–17). Information technology already exists today to mark and manage every person on planet earth via computer chips with unlimited data that will enable total control by the New World Order.

What is the future of the Antichrist? He will be defeated by the hand of God, the defender of Israel. He will be cast alive into the bottomless pit with the False Prophet, who helped him deceive the nations into believing he was god (Revelation 19:20).

How will Israel and the Jewish people be able to finally

identify the Antichrist? They will know by the specific sign that he will repeat the "abomination of desolation" of Antiochus Epiphanes, Titus, and Hadrian.

Jesus' warning to the Jewish people about the time and identity of Antichrist is as follows:

> Then let those who are in Judea flee to the mountains. Let him who is on the housetop not go down to take anything out of his house. And let him who is on the field not go back to get his clothes. But woe to those who are pregnant and to those who are nursing babies in those days! And pray that your flight may not be in winter or on the Sabbath.
>
> (MATTHEW 24:16–20)

This text proves that the Antichrist will come when Jewish law controls Israel. Praying that your flight "may not be on the Sabbath" could only be possible if the Jewish people were living in Israel and the Sabbath laws were in effect. According to Torah, a Jewish person may not walk more than "A Sabbath Day's Journey" except in emergency situations. On *that day,* the exception to the rule applies and the Jewish people may run *any* distance to save their lives.

THE GREAT TRIBULATION

Matthew 24:21 says, "Then [after the Antichrist has committed the abomination of desolation to the Jewish Temple] there will be great tribulation, such as has not been since the beginning of the world until this time, no, nor ever shall be."

Remember that Matthew 24 is a message from a Jewish Rabbi to His twelve Jewish disciples. Jesus says this time of great tribulation will be worse than anything ever experienced in history. When you recall the destruction of Jerusalem by the Babylonians, the million-plus Jews who died when Titus besieged the city in AD 70, the monstrous acts of Hadrian in AD 130, and the systematic slaughter of six million Jews in Hitler's Holocaust, it staggers the mind to grasp a kind of trial and tribulation that would exceed these atrocities. But Jesus, the all-knowing Lord, has said a greater tribulation than these is coming. The prophet Daniel describes this time as "a time of distress, such as never occurred since there was a nation" (12:1 NASB).

Some are teaching that we are currently experiencing the Great Tribulation. Our nation is under God's judgment, but the times we are living in is a Shangri-La compared to what's coming in the Great Tribulation.

We read in Revelation 9:15 that on a certain day during the Great Tribulation one-third of mankind will be killed. Think about it! There are about six billion people on the earth today. Think of two billion people being killed in twenty-four hours around the world!

Revelation 6 describes the red horse of war, the black horse of famine, and the pale horse of death. This *trinity of torment* thunders across the face of the earth, commanded by the Antichrist, who is riding the white horse of Revelation 6:1.

The Bible records that in the final battle for global supremacy at Armageddon, "blood came out of the winepress, up to the horses' bridles, for one thousand six hundred furlongs," or two hundred miles (Revelation 14:20).

This kind of human suffering and massive death toll is beyond the mind of man to fathom and why Jesus Christ, the Son of God, accurately calls it the "great tribulation."

This mega-eradication of lives seemed utterly impossible to comprehend, but with the holocaust that will result from the effects of a global nuclear war, killing two billion people in a day is inevitable.

The nuclear genie is out of the bottle and Armageddon is knocking at the door.

LIGHTNING FROM THE EAST

When Jesus came to earth the first time in Bethlehem, only Mary and Joseph and a handful of shepherds gathered at the manger for the birth of God's Son.

When Jesus comes the second time, as described in Revelation 19:11–16, the whole world will see Him. The Bible reads:

> For as the lightning comes from east and flashes to the west, so also will the coming of the Son of Man be.
>
> (MATTHEW 24:27)

Have you ever been in a lightning storm? The brilliant flash of light rips through the heavens with such a dazzling display none can miss it. It's so brilliant that it blinds the eye.

Darkness will envelop the earth in the latter part of the Tribulation, for the sun, moon, and stars will not give their normal light (Revelation 8:12). This supernatural darkness will be shattered by the breathtaking brilliance of divine glory such as mankind has never witnessed.

Remember, when the followers of Jesus saw Him on resurrection morning, they fell at His feet, and the Roman soldiers guarding the grave fell as dead men from the blinding light. John the Revelator fell at his feet as dead because "His countenance was like the sun shining in its strength" (Revelation 1:16). If you attempt to look directly at the sun in its full strength, which is millions of miles away, it will destroy your eyesight.

When Jesus returns, He will illuminate the heavens.

The book of Revelation declares that the New Jerusalem will have "no need of the sun or of the moon to shine in it, for the glory of God illuminated it. The Lamb is its light. . . . Its gates shall not be shut at all by day (there shall be no night there)" (Revelation 21:23–25).

The King is coming!

But before His triumphant return, there is a score to settle.

ISRAEL'S TORMENTERS

I believe there is a mystery verse in the Olivet Discourse that contains a hidden yet obvious meaning about all the nations that have—or *will*—torment the Jewish people and threaten to bring destruction against the land of Israel, the land of God's promise. We read:

> Wherever the carcass is, there the eagles will be gathered together.
>
> (MATTHEW 24:28)

The *hidden* meaning refers to the two evil empires that tormented the Jewish people beyond any other nations of the earth: the Romans and the Nazis' Third Reich. Both of these nations fought under the flag and symbol of the eagle. Every Roman officer had an eagle on the end of his lance. Titus put an eagle on the Temple in Jerusalem and Hitler's demonic Nazi flag was emblazoned with the image of the eagle.

Rome was responsible for the slaughter of the Jewish people under Titus and Hadrian in Jerusalem. Adolf Hitler's Third Reich systematically slaughtered six million of the chosen people in the death camps of Europe. God Almighty has not forgotten, and He has a special payday for these evil empires.

The next major prophetic war that is coming to the Middle East will be the Gog-Magog War. Among those nations coming against Israel is Germany, who will follow Russia and Iran. They will be joined by Ethiopia, Libya, and Turkey (Ezekiel 38:5–6).

God has not forgotten ancient Persia's (modern day Iran) attempt to annihilate the Jewish people through Haman's plot. He still remembers the abomination of Epiphanes, Titus, and Hadrian. He recalls the pogroms of Russia that slaughtered hundreds of thousands of His beloved chosen. The blood of the six million cries out to Him. And just as Hitler planned a "Final Solution" for the Jewish people, God is planning a final solution for the enemies of Israel.

The prophet Ezekiel makes it very clear—God will kill 84 percent of the Gog-Magog army when they place their feet on the sacred soil of Israel (Ezekiel 39:1–2 KJV). God will do it by stoning from His very hand, with massive earthquakes, and by causing "every man's sword [to] be against his brother" (38:21).

The original Roman Empire will be reborn and be led by the Antichrist into Israel for the Battle of Armageddon, which is the last battle in the book of Revelation. Jesus Christ is going to slaughter the invading armies for their carnage against the Jewish people (Revelation 19:13–15).

Again, this references the *hidden meaning* evidenced by the eagles on the carcass. The carcass speaks of death. The eagles, the translation of which can be "buzzards," represent *all* the nations who tormented Israel.

The *obvious meaning* of Matthew 24:28 is revealed in Revelation 19:17–21, when God Himself is going to invite the birds of the earth to eat the dead flesh of those who have attacked Israel. The Bible describes the scene very graphically:

> Then I saw an angel standing in the sun; and he cried with a loud voice, saying to all the birds that fly in the midst of heaven, "Come and gather together for the supper of the great God, that you may eat the flesh of kings, the flesh of captains, the flesh of mighty men, the flesh of horses and of those who sit on them, and the flesh of all people, free and slave, both small and great." . . . And all the birds were filled with their flesh.
>
> (REVELATION 19:17–18, 21)

The nations that have touched the apple of God's eye—and will attempt to torment them in the future—will be utterly destroyed on the hills of Israel by the God of Abraham, Isaac, and Jacob.

It's going to happen!

Having told His disciples of the Great Tribulation (Matthew 24:15–29), the Rabbi continues His Olivet Discourse by describing the next major event in this prophetic digest of tomorrow's world.

CHAPTER 11
The Second Coming

Then the sign of the Son of Man will appear in heaven, and then all the tribes of the earth will mourn, and they will see the Son of Man coming on the clouds of heaven with power and great glory.

—MATTHEW 24:30

Jesus Christ is coming back the second time to a world living in the unspeakable terror of the Great Tribulation. People are looking for any glimmer of hope; they are even following false prophets in search of their redemption. In desperation, they will believe and spread false reports saying, "Look, He is in the desert" or "Look, He is in the inner rooms!" (Matthew 24:26).

During this time, the false prophet of the Antichrist will be performing miracles, and because of them, deception will be rampant: "to deceive, if possible, even the elect" (v. 24). Christ warns His generation and those generations to come, "Do not believe it" (v. 26). The Rabbi describes His second coming not as someone in the desert, but "as lightning comes from the east and flashes to the west" (v. 27). I believe Jesus will appear first in Jerusalem (the east), and His radiance will reach the west as the sun shining at full strength.

The second coming of Christ will cause "all the tribes of the earth [to] mourn" (v. 30). Why? The vast majority of the people who do not take the mark of the beast will be killed by the Antichrist and many of the people who remain will be demonized disciples of the prince of darkness.

The "tribes of the earth" are the same people who will give celebratory gifts to each other when the prophet Elijah and Enoch are killed in the streets of Jerusalem by the Antichrist (Revelation 11:10). These people are reprobate, God-hating, devil-worshiping servants of the Antichrist who mourn because Jesus Christ is going to destroy the godless kingdom they idolize.

POWER AND GLORY

Jesus said that He will return "on the clouds of heaven with power and great glory" (Matthew 24:30).

The first time He came, He was the Lamb of God slain from the foundations of the earth who opened not His mouth, who was led to the slaughter for your redemption and mine. When He returns the second time, He will be the Lion of Judah who roars and makes the earth tremble with His power and His glory. He will crush the kings of the east (China) and the west (Europe) who will be led by the Antichrist.

The first time He came, He was dragged before Pilate and Herod. The next time He comes, kings and queens, presidents and prime ministers, senators and governors from the nations of the world will line up in Jerusalem to bow before Jesus Christ, the carpenter's son, the Son of King David, a blood descendant of Abraham, Isaac, and Jacob. The Bible says that "every knee should bow . . . and that every tongue should confess that Jesus Christ is Lord, to the glory of God the Father" (Philippians 2:10–11).

The first time He came, He rode a donkey into Jerusalem. The second time He comes He will be mounted on a white stallion, His name will be called Faithful and True, and in righteousness He will judge and make war. His eyes will be as a flame of fire, and on His head will be many crowns. He will be clothed with a robe dipped in the blood of His enemies and the enemies of Israel, and His name will be called the Word of God. The armies that are in heaven, adorned in white linen, will follow Him on white horses.

Out of His mouth goes a sharp sword, which is His spoken Word. He will strike down the nations and will rule them with a rod of iron. He Himself treads the winepress of the fierceness and wrath of God Almighty. And He will have on His robe and on His thigh a name written: KING OF KINGS AND LORD OF LORDS.

(REVELATION 19:15–16)

GATHERING THE ELECT

God created the earth, and as the Owner of planet earth He made a divine covenant with Abraham, Isaac, and Jacob that the land of Israel was theirs forever. From the book of Genesis until this day, tyrants and dictators have done everything in their power to take the land of Israel away from the Jewish people.

The day is soon coming when God Almighty is going to crush the enemies of Israel once and for all. Remember, the references in the Olivet Discourse to "the elect" (Matthew 24:24, 31) refer to the Jewish people—not the church.

The "elect" is the nation that God has chosen, as recorded in the book of Exodus 19:5–6:

"Now therefore, if you [the Jewish people] will indeed obey My voice and keep My covenant, then you shall be a special treasure to Me above all people; for all the earth is Mine. And you shall be to Me a kingdom of priests and a holy nation." These are the words that you shall speak to the children of Israel.

During the Tribulation the Jewish people will be protected by the hand of God at the natural fortress of Petra located in Jordan. When the enemies of Israel are destroyed, God "will send His angels with a great sound of a trumpet, and they will gather together His elect [Jewish people], from one end of heaven to the other" (Matthew 24:31).

During the golden age of peace—the millennial reign—the righteous Gentiles and the Jewish people will be center stage with the Messiah. All others will be cast into outer darkness for eternity. Men will study war no more, and every man shall "beat their swords into plowshares" (Isaiah 2:4). The wolf will not devour the lamb and the kingdom of our God shall endure forever.

> The wolf will live with the lamb, the leopard will lie down with the goat, the calf and the lion and the yearling together; and a little child will lead them.
>
> (ISAIAH 11:6 NIV1984)

Beginning with the study of the signs in the heavens and walking through the Spine of Prophecy, I have attempted to build a scriptural foundation for God's prophetic depiction regarding the coming Four Blood Moons. Without a clear and concise understanding of God's plan, which is revealed in Scripture, then the Four Blood Moons would be nothing more than a spectacular cosmic occurrence as opposed to the fulfillment of prophecy. There is a reason God has alerted us to "look up" for the coming of the Lord.

His return is closer than you think.

Scripture and human history will once again align with the sun, moon, and the stars as we discover the truth of the Four Blood Moons.

Prepare to be amazed!

SECTION 3

THE FOUR BLOOD MOONS

CHAPTER 12

The Four Blood Moons and Two Feasts

I will show wonders in heaven above
And signs in the earth beneath.
Blood and fire and vapor of smoke.
The sun shall be turned into darkness,
And the moon into blood,
Before the coming of the great and
awesome day of the LORD.

—ACTS 2:19–20

I began my search for answers to Pastor Mark's challenging question, "Have you ever considered the sun, moon, and stars in the study of prophecy?"

NASA Discovery

My first attempt was to open the NASA website and search for lunar signals. I'm not a computer whiz. My secretary is; I am not. But she wasn't with me, so I just kept searching and could find nothing to validate the connection of the Four Blood Moons to prophecy.

The Scriptures speak of "signs in the heavens," many of which have been confirmed by NASA. The Bible and America's best scientists are in agreement that planet earth is watching the signs in the heavens that are dramatically increasing in number and intensity. But still, I could not find the connection to prophecy.

Then I thought for a moment and remembered my conversation with Pastor Mark; maybe these lunar signs are meant for Israel. God is the defender of Israel. He created Israel. Israel is His firstborn son (Exodus 4:22). So I chose the first date that came to my mind, which was the year of Israel's rebirth, and typed in the following statement: "Total moon eclipse in 1948."

What I saw in the middle of the computer screen made me literally leap out of my chair.

Four "blood-red" total lunar eclipses will fall on Passover and Sukkot in 2014 and 2015, the same back-to-back occurrences at the time of 1492, 1949 and 1967.[1]

Those three dates were the most important dates in all of Israel's history!

There have been several Tetrads (four consecutive blood moons) since NASA first recorded their occurrences, but Tetrads linked to significant Jewish history have happened only three times in more than five hundred years. These specific occurrences could not be ignored. My further research led me to the unmistakable biblical and scientific truth that they are about to happen a fourth time.

I considered my next step. When I discover a potential new prophetic revelation, I go to the absolute truth of the Word of God, which is the foundation of all sound biblical research and teaching.

THE ABSOLUTE TRUTH

God Almighty is the Creator of heaven and earth. The first chapter of Genesis is the most God-centered chapter in the Bible. God is mentioned by name thirty-two times in thirty-one verses. The statement "God created the heavens and the earth" in Genesis 1:1 sweeps away atheism by asserting God's all-powerful existence. God is! He's not trying to be—*He is!*

From the first word in Genesis to the last in the book of Revelation, there is one God.

He's the God of Abraham, Isaac, and Jacob. He is the One who scooped up a handful of dirt, breathed into it, and allowed man to become a living soul. He is the One who sent

His Son to die on the cross for our redemption. He is the One who holds the seven seas in the palm of His hand. He is the God who created Israel (Genesis 12) and He is the Defender of Israel (Zechariah 12:8).

> Hear, O Israel: the LORD our God, the LORD is one!
>
> (DEUTERONOMY 6:4)

This statement sweeps away polytheism, which is the worship of many gods. The apostle Paul described today's society when he wrote:

> In the last days . . . men will be lovers of themselves, lovers of money, boasters, proud, blasphemous, disobedient to parents, unthankful, unholy, unloving, unforgiving, slanderers, without self-control, brutal, despisers of good, traitors, headstrong, haughty, lovers of pleasure rather than lovers of God, having a form of godliness but denying its power. And from such people turn away!
>
> (2 TIMOTHY 3:1–5)

The world has taken a wrong turn and we need a sign from God to get back on the right track—the Four Blood Moons just may be that signal!

If God gave Joshua and Hezekiah a sign in the heavens

and if He posted a sign in the heavens to direct the wise men to the birthplace of our Redeemer, then why wouldn't He continue to speak to us through signs? God is the same yesterday, today, and forever, and He has declared that He will give the terminal generation a signal that something big—*something earthshaking*—is going to happen.

He is the God who flung the glittering stars against the velvet of the night. He calls by name the stars that we have yet to locate even with the sophistication of the Hubble telescope. It is a fact that the Creator of heaven and earth is in control of the universe and He is giving us signs in the heavens to alert us of things to come. The question is, "Are we watching?"

THE FEASTS OF THE LORD

In my book *His Glory Revealed* I explain the scriptural applications of the seven Feasts of Israel by giving their relevant historical account and their prophetic interpretations.

The Feasts of the Lord (Festivals) are intended to draw the minds and hearts of the people toward God, they are a time of sweet communion and joy, and, finally, they illustrate profound spiritual truths that create a portrait of God's master plan for the ages. Through these festivals, God is giving us a depiction of what He has already done as well as a prophetic portrait of what is coming in the years ahead.

The Hebrew word for *feast* is *mo'ed*, denoting "a set or appointed time." A very similar meaning is *mikrah* indicating a "rehearsal or recital." Each feast, like a dress rehearsal, offers a significant glimpse of God's prophetic plan. The combined feasts, divinely established shortly after the Israelites were redeemed from Egypt's bondage, would be a spiritual blueprint of what lies ahead for Israel, Jerusalem, and the rest of the world.

All Jewish holidays begin the evening before the date specified on most calendars. This is because a Jewish "day" begins and ends at sunset, rather than at midnight like the Gregorian calendar.

If you read the story of creation in Genesis 1, you will notice that it records, "And there was evening, and there was morning, one day." From this, we conclude that a day begins with evening and ends the following evening; that is, sunset to sunset.

As I present the significance of the Four Blood Moons in the chapters to follow, I will mention two feasts that are directly associated with their past and future occurrences. In order to better understand their noteworthy connection, I will briefly describe them; they are Passover (Pesach) and the Feast of Tabernacles (Sukkot).

PASSOVER

Passover (Pesach) begins on the 15th day of the Jewish month of Nissan. It is the first of the two major festivals with both historical and agricultural significance that occur in the Tetrad.

These are the feasts of the Lord, holy convocations which you shall proclaim at their appointed times. On the fourteenth day of the first month at twilight is the Lord's Passover.

(LEVITICUS 23:4–5)

So this day shall be to you a memorial; and you shall keep it as a feast to the Lord throughout your generations. You shall keep it as a feast by an everlasting ordinance.

(EXODUS 12:14)

Agriculturally, it represents the beginning of the harvest season in Israel, but the primary observances of Pesach are related to the Exodus from Egypt after generations of slavery (Exodus, chapters 1–15).

The name *Pesach* comes from the Hebrew root *Pei-Samekh-Cheit*, meaning to pass through, to pass over, to exempt, or to spare. It refers to the fact that God "passed over" the houses of the Jewish people that applied the lamb's blood on the doorposts of their home as He slayed the firstborn of Egypt. *Pesach* is also the name of the sacrificial offering (a lamb) that was made in the Temple on this holiday.

The moment John the Baptist saw Jesus, he exclaimed, "Behold! The Lamb of God who takes away the sin of the world!" (John 1:29). Jesus fulfilled the meaning of the Passover ritual, for He *is* God's male lamb without spot or blemish (1 Peter 1:19). Jesus, our Passover Lamb, will yet appear a second time.

John the Revelator looked upon heaven's throne room and chronicled the following scene in Revelation 5:

Then I saw a Lamb, looking as if it had been slain, standing at the center of the throne, encircled by the four living creatures and the elders. . . . And when he had taken it, the four living creatures and the twenty-four elders fell down before the Lamb. . . . And they sang a new song, saying:

"You are worthy to take the scroll
and to open its seals,
because you were slain,
and with your blood you purchased for God persons
from every tribe and language and people and nation.
You have made them to be a kingdom and priests
to serve our God,
and they will reign on the earth."

Then I looked and heard the voice of many angels, numbering thousands upon thousands, and ten thousand times ten thousand. They encircled the throne and the living creatures and the elders. In a loud voice they were saying:

"Worthy is the Lamb, who was slain,
   to receive power and wealth and wisdom
   and strength
and honor and glory and praise!"

Then I heard every creature in heaven and on earth
and under the earth and on the sea, and all that is in
them, saying:

"To him who sits on the throne and to the Lamb
   be praise and honor and glory and power,
   for ever and ever!"

(vv. 6–13 NIV)

The Feast of Passover is a time of redemption.

Remember this truth: if you do not understand the pro-
phetical significance of the Feasts of the Lord it's like breaking
the hands off your clock—how will you be able to tell the *appointed time*?

THE FEAST OF TABERNACLES

The Festival of Tabernacles (Sukkot) begins on the 15th day of
the Jewish month of Tishri. The word *Sukkot* means "booths"
and refers to the temporary dwellings that the Jewish people
are commanded to live in during this holiday to commemo-
rate the forty-year period during which the children of Israel

were wandering in the desert, living in temporary shelters.

> Say to the Israelites: "On the fifteenth day of the sev-
> enth month the LORD's Feast of Tabernacles begins,
> and it lasts for seven days. The first day is a sacred as-
> sembly; do no regular work. For seven days present
> offerings made to the LORD by fire, and on the eighth
> day hold a sacred assembly and present an offering
> made to the LORD by fire. . . ." So beginning with the
> fifteenth day of the seventh month, after you have
> gathered the crops of the land, celebrate the festival to
> the LORD for seven days; the first day is a day of rest,
> and the eighth day also is a day of rest. On the first day
> you are to take choice fruit from the trees, and palm
> fronds, leafy branches and poplars, and rejoice before
> the LORD your God for seven days. Celebrate this as a
> festival to the LORD for seven days each year. This is
> to be a lasting ordinance for the generations to come;
> celebrate it in the seventh month. Live in booths for
> seven days: All native-born Israelites are to live in
> booths so your descendants will know that I had the
> Israelites live in booths when I brought them out of
> Egypt. I am the LORD your God.
>
> (LEVITICUS 23:34–43 NIV1984)

Agriculturally, Sukkot is a harvest festival and is sometimes referred to as the Festival of Ingathering. It is so unreservedly joyful that it is commonly referred as the "Season of Our Rejoicing."² The Feast of Tabernacles is ultimately a time of thanksgiving for God's provision.

The Festival of Sukkot is the rehearsal dinner for the millennial reign of Christ. For the first time Israel will possess all the land promised to Abraham in Genesis 15:18–21. Jerusalem, the apple of God's eye, will become the joy of the world, for Jesus will reign there. The Millennium will be a time of rest for the people of God (Hebrew 4:8–9). The prophet Isaiah echoes the thought: "In that day the Root of Jesse will stand as a banner for the peoples; the nations will rally to him, and his place of rest will be glorious" (Isaiah 11:10 NIV1984).

The Feast of Tabernacles is a time of remembrance, rejoicing, and rest.

CHAPTER 13

The Four Blood Moons of 1493–94

The sun will be turned to darkness
and the moon to blood
before the coming of the great and dreadful day of the Lord.

—Joel 2:31 NIV

As I have stated, three Tetrads that are specifically linked to Jewish history have appeared in the past five hundred years. Each Tetrad series, consisting of four consecutive Blood Moons with a total solar eclipse occurring somewhere within the sequence of the total lunar eclipses, announced a time of tears and tribulation that would end in national triumph for the Jewish people.

In 1493–94, the first Tetrad of Blood Moons occurred on the Jewish holidays of Passover and Feast of Tabernacles:

1. Passover, April 2, 1493
2. Feast of Tabernacles, September 25, 1493
3. Passover, March 22, 1494
4. Feast of Tabernacles, September 15, 1494

The Four Blood Moons graphics in this chapter and the rest to follow were inspired by *The Feasts of the Lord* DVD set by Mark Biltz of El Shaddai Ministries.[1]

BLOOD MOONS OF 1493–94

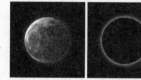

Passover	Total Solar Eclipse	Feast of Tabernacles	Passover	Feast of Tabernacles
April 2, 1493	September 24, 1493	September 25, 1493	March 22, 1494	September 15, 1494

The first Blood Moon in the Tetrad appeared on April 2, 1493—on the first day of Passover after the Jewish events of 1492. There was a total solar eclipse on September 24, 1493—one day before the blood moon of the Feast of Tabernacles, September 25, 1493.

What was happening to the Jewish people during this time?

KING FERDINAND AND QUEEN ISABELLA

Ferdinand II, also known as Ferdinand the Catholic, was king of Aragon and Castile from 1479 to 1516, where he ruled with his wife, Queen Isabella I. They consolidated their power by uniting the Spanish kingdoms into the nation of Spain and began Spain's entry into the modern period of imperial expansion.

In 1481, fear of Jewish influence led Queen Isabella and King Ferdinand to pressure Pope Sixtus IV to allow a monarchy-controlled Inquisition in Spain by threatening to withdraw military support at a time when the Turks were a peril to Rome.[2] Their request was granted and in 1483 the Dominican confessor of Queen Isabella was appointed Inquisitor General of Spain; his name was Tomas de Torquemada. Through his villainous acts of torture the Spanish Inquisition ultimately surpassed the Medieval Inquisition of 1233 in scope, intensity, and atrocities.

Torquemada quickly established malicious and cruel procedures for the Spanish Inquisition. A new court was announced with a thirty-day grace period for confessions and the gathering of accusations by neighbors. Evidence that was used to identify a crypto-Jew (secretly observant) included the absence of chimney smoke on Saturdays (a sign the family might secretly be honoring the Sabbath) or the buying of many vegetables before Passover or the purchase of meat from a converted butcher.

The Inquisition's court employed physical torture to extract confessions. Crypto-Jews were allowed to confess and do penance, although those who relapsed were burned at the stake.[3]

The Medieval Inquisition originated years before as a Roman Catholic tribunal for the discovery and punishment of heresy. It was created under Pope Innocent III of Rome (1198–1216) and later established under Pope Gregory IX in 1233.[4]

Anti-Semitism sponsored by the Roman Church began to manifest itself openly in 1412, when Jews were told they would have to live in separate quarters. These isolated quarters were the later template of the Polish ghettos established by the Nazis (1939–42) and the Minsk Ghetto of Russia (1941–43).[5]

In addition to being forced to live in the ghettos, the Jewish people were told they must distinguish themselves from Christians by allowing their beards to grow out and wearing the yellow Star of David on their clothing. The Jews could no longer hold public office, could not be physicians, and could not lend their money with interest. All schools and professions were closed to the Jewish people, and all commerce by which they might make a living was prohibited.[6]

This was only the beginning of the persecution, torture, and death of the Jewish people by the Roman Church's Inquisitors. In less than twelve years the Inquisition condemned no fewer than thirteen thousand Jews, men and women who had continued to practice Judaism in secret.[7]

I now take you back to King Ferdinand and Queen Isabella

who established and controlled the Spanish Inquisition. The monarchy took increasingly drastic measures against the Jews and on March 30, 1492, at their palace in Granada, King Ferdinand and Queen Isabella signed a decree ordering the Jews to leave Castile and Aragon by August 1. This was known as the Edict of Expulsion, which banished all Jewish people from Spain who refused to convert to Catholicism.

The ousted Jews were stripped of their wealth, for the Edict prohibited them from taking gold, silver, and precious metals. More than poverty, however, the decree meant homelessness and uncertainty, since the Jews did not know which nations would receive them. They also feared the journey, which would bring death to those too weak to endure it.

Christopher Columbus recorded this infamous edict in his diary:

In the same month in which their Majesties [Ferdinand and Isabella] issued the edict that all Jews should be driven out of the kingdom and its territories, in the same month they gave me the order to undertake with sufficient men my expedition of discovery to the Indies.

The expulsion that Columbus refered to was so cataclysmic an event that since then, the year 1492 has been almost as important in Jewish history as in American history. On July 30 of that year, the entire Jewish community that had not been converted or killed—some 200,000—were expelled from Spain.[8]

The Jews were given the date of August 1 as the deadline for their departure from Spain, but some left the following day, August 2, which was the 9th of Av (*Tishah b'Av*) on the Jewish calendar. *Tishah b'Av* is a fast day that commemorates the destruction of the first and second temples; once again, remember a Jewish day begins and ends at sunset.

The following day, Christopher Columbus and his expedition set sail out of the harbor near Seville, past the ships upon which Jewish exiles were embarking. His voyage of discovery was financed by money confiscated from the Jewish people.[9]

I call to the witness stand of history the scholar Dagobert D. Runes, who recorded the brutal and godless acts of torture upon the Jews of Spain during the Spanish Inquisition by those who called themselves *Christians*.

> The Spanish Inquisition was perhaps the most cynical plot in the dark history of Catholicism, aimed at expropriating the property of well-to-do Jews and converts in Spain, for the benefit of the royal court and the Church. Even dead "suspects" had their bones dug up for "trial" so estates could be confiscated from their heirs.[10]

> Solemn ritualistic burning of Jews and other "heretics"

at the behest of the inquisitional authorities of the Catholic Church began. "Trials" were conducted in the presence of the clergy and invariably ended in confession under torture by fire, skinning alive, bone-crushing, etc. The verdict was almost always; "burn them alive."[11]

The infamous "blood libel" tale was employed by the Inquisitors to justify the torture of the Jews of Spain. The blood libel had at its root the rumor that a Christian child had been killed by Jews and his blood used to celebrate Passover.

In Avila, a Spanish town near Madrid in 1491 a child from "La Guardia," a village that never existed was allegedly found dead. A Jewish shoemaker, his brother and father were accused by the Church of having killed the child (later canonized) and drinking its blood for Passover. The accused admitted, under torture, all points of the indictment. Following their burning, all Jews in this little town were murdered and their homes sacked. The Catholic clergy appropriated the synagogue for a church.[12]

In the town of Seville, Fernando Martinez, who was archdeacon of the town, mobilized the people in a massacre against the Jewish quarter. A total of four thousand Jews were killed, and the townspeople forced the remainder to enroll in their so-called *religion of love!* These church-sponsored pogroms spread throughout Spain. Runes writes, "Synagogues were converted, together with pitifully few Jewish survivors, to the 'Truth Faith.' In some ghettos, not a single Jew survived, and the local Christians had their new 'House of God' to themselves."[13]

Elinor and Robert Slater write about a long night of anti-Semitism in their book, *Great Moments in Jewish History*:

Any Jew who observed Jewish customs, even the "wearing of clean clothes on the Jewish Sabbath," became suspect and were brought before the Inquisitors for trial. Some were fined; others suffered confiscation of property and torture. The rack was used not only to extract confessions from the accused but to force them to inform against others. Many of the accused were put to death in theatrical executions staged in public squares of Spanish towns. An execution of this type, usually by fire was known as auto-da-fe, or act of faith.[14]

The Jewish community in Spain tried desperately to have the Edict of Expulsion repealed. A delegation consisting of Abraham Senior and Isaac Abravanel obtained an audience with King Ferdinand and Queen Isabella. Senior, the Chief Rabbi of Castile, was, in effect, the leader of Spanish Jewry.

Isaac Abravanel, a scholar and philosopher, was the financial adviser whose skill had enabled Spain to conquer Granada.

They appealed to the king and queen for mercy, and to strengthen their case they offered a substantial payment in exchange for revocation of the decree. According to one version of this meeting, the delegation placed the bag of money on the table.

Moved both by the power of their arguments and by the sight of the gold, Ferdinand and Isabella hesitated. "Just then, the Grand Inquisitor, Thomas de Torquemada, entered the room. He approached the table, set the cross he held in his hand near the bag of gold, and said, pointing to the figure of Jesus on the cross, 'Here He is, sell Him!' The royal couple's doubts vanished. They rejected the delegation's pleas and ordered the Jews to prepare for departure."[15]

Lest we believe that anti-Semitism was exclusive to the Roman church, let me direct you to Martin Luther (1483–1586), the primary leader of the Protestant Reformation.

Having been disillusioned by the corruption of the Roman church, Luther turned to Scripture for solace. He discovered that salvation comes through faith in Christ and not through Rome. After being excommunicated by the Church and marked as a "convicted heretic" for his vocal and written criticisms of its doctrines, Luther went into hiding where he translated the New Testament into German, giving the "common people" the opportunity to benefit from its truths.

Luther initially was a friend of the Jews, writing that "treating the Jews in an unfriendly way was unchristian." He truly believed that his revelation of salvation through grace would appeal to the Jewish people. However, when his efforts to convert them failed, Luther became angry and vindictive. He subsequently wrote a pamphlet, *Against the Jews and Their Lies.*

Luther declared the Jews as "public enemies" and beseeched that the Church and civil leaders take action against the Jewish people. Among his evil recommendations: (1) burn synagogues and Jewish schools, (2) raze and destroy Jewish homes, (3) take their prayer books and Talmudic writings, (4) forbid Rabbis to teach, (5) take their silver and gold, (6) make them work for their keep.

Martin Luther's *Against the Jews and Their Lies* was a blueprint for "Kristallnacht," so much so that in honor of Luther's works, the first synagogues were burned on his birthday. Many believe Hitler's "Final Solution" was inspired by Luther's written works, which embodied his vile hatred against the Jewish people.

Why were the Jewish people segregated, tortured, killed, and banished?

For one reason and one reason only: they were a people who would not convert from their belief in the One God of Abraham, Isaac, and Jacob. Remember, as I said in chapter 1, it may have been called *Christianity* for hundreds of years, but the acts of the Inquisition had *nothing* to do with *Christianity*.

They had nothing to do with the love of God. They were *not* connected to our Savior and Lord. These villainous acts were nothing more than religious tyranny. They were the acts of pious church leaders whose souls had been poisoned with the evil seed of anti-Semitism. The Inquisition should never be labeled as one that was sanctioned by the message of Jesus Christ. Never!

A Harbor of Refuge

God caused Christopher Columbus to discover the "new world," which would eventually become America, a refuge to the Jewish people and all who were oppressed by tyrants and religious dictators around the world.

God had promised Abraham centuries before in Genesis 12:3,

I will bless those who bless you,
And I will curse him who curses you;
And in you all the families of the earth shall be blessed.

God has blessed America because we opened our arms to the seed of Abraham who have blessed the world beyond measure. I believe the day America turns its back on Israel and the Jewish people will be the exact day in history when God Almighty lifts His hand of blessing from America. The policies of our present government are putting daylight between

Washington and Israel. Beware, America! God is watching! His honor and integrity rest upon His supernatural defense of Israel.

Israel is the only nation in the history of the world created by a sovereign act of God. God, the Creator of heaven and earth, entered into a real estate covenant with Abraham, Isaac, and Jacob that the land of Israel would be theirs forever (Genesis 13:14–15; 17:7–8). Israel must never be separated from this ancient Bible covenant.

God continued His proclamation concerning Abraham and the Jewish people, saying, "I will curse him who curses you" (Genesis 12:3). The era of King Ferdinand and Queen Isabella's reign in Spain before the expulsion of the Jews is recorded in history as the Spanish Golden Age. The prosperity of Spain plummeted after the Jews were expelled and has never recovered.

Ever since the Edict of Expulsion, Spain has been ruled by dictators and despots, and today is facing national bankruptcy. In the twenty-first century, Spain is controlled by radical Islamists who blow up their trains and plot the death of anyone who dares to resist them.[16] The irony cannot be ignored—the Jews who were expelled from Spain were a people who loved life. The radical Islamists love death. Spain is experiencing the curse of Genesis 12:3!

God continues His proclamation to Abraham, stating, "And in you [the Jewish people] all the families of the earth shall be blessed" (Genesis 12:3). Every person reading this book has been blessed by the contributions that the Jewish people have given to the world. As we have stated, the Jewish people have given us the Bible, the patriarchs, the first family of Christianity, and the apostles. Christianity cannot explain its existence without Judaism. That's why our faith is referred as the *Judeo-Christian faith*. Our roots are found in Abraham, Isaac, and Jacob.

The Spanish Inquisition was a time of tears and tribulation that would end in triumph for the Jewish people as God brought them to America's harbor of protection.

The expulsion of the Jews from Spain in 1492 was a world-changing moment. The mantle of prosperity was lifted from Spain and placed upon the shoulders of an infant nation that would become the United States of America. God Almighty used the Four Blood Moons of 1493–94 as a *heavenly billboard* to mankind.

Now let us explore the meaning of the Four Blood Moons of 1949–50 when miraculously, after two thousand years, Israel became a state.

CHAPTER 14

The Four Blood Moons of 1949–50

I will take you from among the nations,
gather you out of all countries, and bring you into
your own land. . . . Then you shall dwell in the land
that I gave to your fathers; you shall be My people,
and I will be your God.

—EZEKIEL 36:24, 28

The second appearance of Four Blood Moons that are significantly linked to Jewish history was reported by NASA during 1949–50.[1] They occurred during the rebirth of the State
of Israel, which began in 1948. The mighty right hand of God
gathered the Jewish people who, beginning in AD 70, had

been scattered across the earth when Titus besieged Jerusalem. The Jewish people of the Diaspora were brought back to Israel, just as the Old Testament prophets had prophesied.

This Tetrad, beginning in 1949, occurred on the Jewish holidays of Passover and the Feast of Tabernacles:

1. Passover, April 13, 1949
2. Feast of Tabernacles, October 7, 1949
3. Passover, April 2, 1950
4. Feast of Tabernacles, September 26, 1950

BLOOD MOONS OF 1949–50

Passover	Feast of Tabernacles	Passover	**Total Solar Eclipse**	Feast of Tabernacles
April 13, 1949	October 7, 1949	April 2, 1950	**September 12, 1950**	September 26, 1950

A total solar eclipse took place on September 12, 1950, before the Feast of Tabernacles on September 26.

What was happening to the Jewish people during this time?

It was in 1948 that Israel was once again declared a nation. There is no greater miracle in human history than the miracle of the ingathering of the seed of Abraham. The Land of Israel was the birthplace of the Jewish people. The Land of Israel was where their spiritual identity was shaped. The Land of Israel is where the Jewish people will reside forever.

After being forcibly exiled by Titus in AD 70 the Jewish people never lost their love and connection to their sacred land. Throughout the Diaspora they never ceased to hope for the restoration of their national identity and freedom. Their constant prayer was, "Next year in Jerusalem."

Compelled by the Abrahamic covenant and as a result of the horrors of the Spanish Inquisition and Holocaust, the Jewish people endeavored in reestablishing themselves in their ancient homeland more than ever. They returned to the Land as pioneers or *ma'pilim*, which were immigrants coming to Eretz-Israel (the Land of Israel) in defiance of restrictive legislation. They committed themselves to make the deserts bloom, to revive the Hebrew language, to build villages and towns, all the while ready to defend themselves from the enemies that were dedicated to their destruction.

These were peace-loving people who desired nothing more than independent nationhood which would open the gates of their biblical homeland to every Jewish person scattered among the nations.

THEODORE HERZL—THE VISIONARY

In 1897, Theodore Herzl, who is known as the founder of Zionism, convened the First Zionist Congress and proclaimed the right of the Jewish people to national rebirth in their own country. This right was recognized in the Balfour Declaration of November 1917 and reaffirmed in the Mandate of the League of Nations, which specifically gave international sanction to the historic connection between the Jewish people and Eretz-Israel (Land of Israel) and to the right of the Jewish people to rebuild their national homeland.

Herzl was motivated by his personal experience of anti-Semitism while studying at the university in Vienna and, specifically, the trial of Captain Alfred Dreyfus in 1894. Dreyfus, a Jewish officer in the French army, was unjustly accused of treason, primarily because of the predominant anti-Semitic atmosphere in Vienna. Herzl witnessed mobs shouting, "Death to the Jews" and resolved that there was only one solution: the mass immigration of Jews to a land that they could call their own. This was the genesis of Zionism, the national movement for the return of the Jewish people to their covenant homeland and the resumption of Jewish sovereignty.[2]

MENACHEM BEGIN—THE WARRIOR

Menachem Begin was a Jewish youth leader in Poland when the Russians invaded during World War II. He was captured and placed in prison, where he was interrogated every night for hours. He slept in a cell infected by fleas. I will never forget him saying to me, "The first flea is considered an invader, and the rest are considered welcomed friends."

After Begin's release, he immediately traveled to what was then called *Palestine* (named after WWI for territories under the British Mandate, which included not only present-day Israel but also present-day Jordan). It was a time when Britain was decidedly pro-Arab. However, due to the Balfour Declaration, the governed body was forced to allow Jews to immigrate to Palestine. But they limited the number of immigrants by creating the harsh White Paper policy of 1939. This policy was decidedly influenced by the Arabs and limited the number of Jewish immigrants into Palestine to a meager ten thousand per year.

Here's the problem: this was during the Holocaust when Hitler was sending twenty thousand Jews per day to the concentration camps of Europe. The Jews who were privileged to receive immigration documents to Palestine had a ticket to life; those who did not were at first put in ghettos and then sent to the camps where they were treated like animals by the demonized anti-Semitic Nazis. Making matters worse, the British army rounded up any Jewish person without immigration documents who managed to get to Palestine and then sent them back to Hitler's death camps.[3]

When Menachem Begin arrived in Palestine and witnessed the British army put Jews by the hundreds on the trains back to Europe and to Hitler's death camps, he decided to form the paramilitary group known as the Irgun. The word *Irgun* in Hebrew means "our group." The purpose of the Irgun was to teach Jewish men how to fight and liberate their fellow Jews from the trains and ships headed for Hitler's death camps.

Under the radar of British intelligence, the Irgun imported the machinery to manufacture their own rifles and ammunition. The Irgun also developed a percussion bomb that was placed on the train tracks. When the train, loaded with captured Jews bound for the death camps, would pass over the percussion bomb, it was timed to blow up between the engine and the coal car. It cut the train like a knife. The engine sailed down the tracks, the cars slowed down, and Menachem's Irgun boarded the trains and liberated their fellow Jews.

The British put out a very lucrative bounty for the capture of Menachem Begin. Begin's resolve became as steel while he was in the Russian prisons. On one occasion, he hid in the fireplace of his home for three days straight while the British Intelligence officers interrogated his wife who was just a few feet away. He may have looked like a bespectacled mild-mannered schoolteacher, but he was a dedicated warrior and liberator of the Jewish people.

The King David Hotel was the command center for the British army with approximately three hundred British officers and soldiers living on the premises. Menachem Begin and the Irgun wired the King David Hotel with explosives. The British commander was then called by phone and given the opportunity to evacuate the hotel prior to the explosion.

The British commanding officer vigorously refused to obey the orders of a Jew and believed the call to be a prank. The Irgun then detonated a small bomb in the middle of the street in front of the hotel to demonstrate it was no hoax.

The British still refused to leave the King David Hotel. The explosives were set off and several hundred British soldiers needlessly perished.[4]

Menachem Begin was characterized as a terrorist. Not so! He was committed to saving the lives of the Jewish people. He was eventually rewarded by the people of Israel when they elected him prime minister. It was my pleasure to meet with him several times during his very successful administration. In fact, I have his autographed picture hanging on my study wall.

He was a devout man who studied the Torah every day. After his term in office, he taught a Bible class in his home every Friday night. I believe that without Menachem Begin and his Irgun organization the British would not have left Palestine and thousands more Jewish lives would have been lost to the Holocaust.

When you go to Israel, I encourage you to visit the Menachem Begin Museum. There you will fully appreciate the heroic exploits of this fearless man and you will better understand the urgent compulsion of the Jewish people to reestablish the nation of Israel. May God bless the sacred memory of this dedicated defender of Israel.

DAVID BEN-GURION—THE DIPLOMAT

Ben-Gurion was a Zionist statesman and political leader, the first prime minister (1948–53, 1955–63) and defense minister (1948–53, 1955–63) of Israel.

It was Ben-Gurion who delivered Israel's declaration of independence in Tel Aviv on May 14, 1948. His charismatic personality won him the adoration of the masses; he was revered as the "Father of the Nation."

In 1906 the twenty-year-old Ben-Gurion immigrated to Palestine and worked as a farmer in the Jewish agricultural settlements for several years. As the Jewish settlement strengthened and deepened its roots in Palestine, anxiety mounted among the Palestinian Arabs, resulting in violent clashes between the two communities.

Ben-Gurion reacted to the British White Paper Policy of 1939 by calling upon the Jewish community to rise against the British and on May 12, 1942, he assembled an emergency conference of American Zionists in New York City where the convention decided upon the establishment of a Jewish commonwealth in Palestine after the war.[5]

At the end of World War II, Ben-Gurion again led the Jewish community in its successful struggle against the British mandate; and in May 1948, in accordance with a decision of the United Nations General Assembly, and with the support of the United States, the State of Israel was established. The Declaration of Statehood read in part:

ACCORDINGLY WE, Members of The People's Council, Representatives of The Jewish Community of Eretz-Israel And of The Zionist Movement, Are Here Assembled On The Day of The Termination of The British Mandate Over Eretz-Israel And, By Virtue of Our Natural And Historic Right And On The Strength of The Resolution of The United Nations General Assembly, Hereby Declare The Establishment of A Jewish State In Eretz-Israel, To Be Known As The State of Israel....

Placing Our Trust In The Almighty, We Affix Our Signatures To This Proclamation At This Session Of The Provisional Council Of State, On The Soil Of The Homeland, In The City of Tel-Aviv, On This Sabbath Eve The 5th Day Of Iyar, 5708—14th May, 1948.[6]

Ben-Gurion viewed the newborn state as the direct continuation of Jewish history that had been interrupted two thousand years earlier when the Roman legions had crushed the Hebrew freedom fighters and banished the Jews from their land. He saw the Jews' period of exile as a prolonged interlude in the history of Israel and declared that they had now regained their rightful home. David Ben-Gurion believed that Israel was "a country built more on her people ... the Jews will come from everywhere ... from France, from Russia, from

America and from Yemen . . . their faith is their passport." [7]

Israel was reborn in the month of Iyar—the "second month" has always held great biblical significance. It was in the *second month* that King Solomon began to build the First Temple (1 Kings 6:1); it was in the *second month*, on the same exact day, that Ezra began to rebuild the Second Temple (Ezra 3:8). And it was in the second month on the 5th day of Iyar, that Israel was reborn as a nation.

> Who has ever heard of such things?
> Who has ever seen things like this?
> Can a country be born in a day
> or a nation be brought forth in a moment?
> Yet no sooner is Zion in labor
> than she gives birth to her children.
>
> (ISAIAH 66:8 NIV)

The first permanent Israeli government took office on January 25, 1949. During the next several months, a series of four Israeli War of Independence truce agreements were signed: with Egypt on February 24, with Lebanon on March 23, with Jordan on April 3, and with Syria on July 20. All of these agreements created armistice demarcation lines, which established Israel's borders.[8]

It was during this process of Israel's rebirth and the establishment of her borders that on Passover 1949 God splattered the heavens with the first Blood Moon of the second Tetrad. The Jewish people had endured the severe tribulation of the Holocaust, the trials of rebirthing a nation, and now it was a time of triumph; they were officially home and home forever.

The Jews had returned to the covenant land of Israel but something was missing. The third series of Four Blood Moons would signal the complete restoration of their beloved capital, the city of God.

CHAPTER 15

The Four Blood Moons of 1967–68

Yet I have chosen Jerusalem,

that My name may be there.

—2 CHRONICLES 6:6

The third occurrence of a Tetrad of Blood Moons significant to Jewish history, as reported by NASA, was in 1967–68. Why was this significant to Jewish history? 1967 was the year the city of Jerusalem was reunited with the Jewish people for the first time in nearly nineteen hundred years.

This was a monumental prophetic event and God lit up the heavens in celebration of what took place; for Jerusalem is unlike any other city on the face of the earth . . . it is the city of God.

BLOOD MOONS OF 1967–68

The Tetrad of Blood Moons of 1967–68 occurred on the Jewish holidays of Passover and the Feast of Tabernacles:

1. Passover, April 24, 1967
2. Feast of Tabernacles, October 18, 1967
3. Passover, April 13, 1968
4. Feast of Tabernacles, October 6, 1968

BLOOD MOONS OF 1967–68

| Passover April 24, 1967 | Feast of Tabernacles October 18, 1967 | **Total Solar Eclipse November 2, 1967** | Passover April 13, 1968 | Feast of Tabernacles October 6, 1968 |

This third Tetrad, beginning in 1967, occurred on the Jewish holidays of Passover and the Feast of Tabernacles with the total solar eclipse occurring on November 2, 1967, before Passover of 1968.

What was happening to the Jewish people during this time?

THE PRICE OF INDEPENDENCE

See how your enemies growl,

how your foes rear their heads.

With cunning they conspire against your people;

they plot against those you cherish.

"Come," they say, "let us destroy them as a nation,

so that Israel's name is remembered no more."

(PSALM 83:2–4 NIV)

Israel was at war from the moment they declared statehood.

The War of Independence of May 15, 1948, through March 10, 1949, occurred the day after Israel's rebirth. Seven Arab nations came against the apple of God's eye. The war was fought along the entire length of the country's border; against Lebanon and Syria in the north; Iraq and Transjordan in the east; Egypt, assisted by contingents from the Sudan, in the south; and Palestinians and volunteers from Arab countries in the interior of Israel.

It was the bloodiest of Israel's wars with a total of 6,373 killed in action. The jubilant celebration of the nation's rebirth was over. Sandwiched between the War of Independence and the Six-Day War was the Sinai War of October 29 through November 7, 1956, which was fought against Egypt over the control of the strategic Sinai Peninsula.

In 1967, the Arab nations, committed to driving the Jewish

people into the sea, once again rallied against Israel. On May 15, as Israel commemorated their Independence Day, the buildup of Egyptian troops began moving into the Sinai near the Israeli border. By May 18, Syrian troops were prepared for battle along the Golan Heights.

The *growling* voices that King David prophesied concerning Israel's enemies echoed through the airwaves.

On May 18, 1967, The Voice of the Arabs radio station proclaimed:

> As of today, there no longer exists an international emergency force to protect Israel. We shall exercise patience no more. We shall not complain any more to the UN about Israel. The sole method we shall apply against Israel is total war, which will result in the extermination of Zionist existence.[1]

On May 20, Syrian Defense Minister Hafez Assad threatened Israel with the following declaration:

> Our forces are now entirely ready not only to repulse the aggression, but to initiate the act of liberation itself, and to explode the Zionist presence in the Arab homeland. The Syrian army, with its finger on the trigger, is united. . . . I, as a military man, believe that the time has come to enter into a battle of annihilation.[2]

On May 27, Nasser of Egypt challenged Israel:

> "Our basic objective will be the destruction of Israel. The Arab people want to fight," he said.[3] . . . The following day, he added: "We will not accept any . . . coexistence with Israel."[4]

On May 30, King Hussein of Jordan signed a defense pact with Egypt. Nasser then announced:

> The armies of Egypt, Jordan, Syria and Lebanon are poised on the borders of Israel . . . to face the challenge, while standing behind us are the armies of Iraq, Algeria, Kuwait, Sudan and the whole Arab nation. This act will astound the world. Today they will know that the Arabs are arranged for battle, the critical hour has arrived. We have reached the stage of serious action and not declarations.[5]

President Abdur Rahman Aref of Iraq joined in the vicious war of words:

> The existence of Israel is an error which must be rectified. This is our opportunity to wipe out the ignominy which has been with us since 1948. Our goal is clear—to wipe Israel off the map.[6]

On June 4, Iraq joined the military alliance of Egypt, Jordan, and Syria.

The Arab rhetoric was matched by the mobilization of hostile Arab forces. Approximately 465,000 enemy troops, with more than 2,800 tanks, and 800 aircraft surrounded Israel.[7]

THE HAND OF GOD

He did this so that all the peoples of the earth might know that the hand of the LORD is powerful and so that you might always fear the LORD your God.

(JOSHUA 4:24 NIV)

The Six-Day War was a war of miracles. God gave Israel triumph after triumph against their ancient enemies that had occupied their land and divided the sacred city of Jerusalem for centuries. There was no military reason for their victory; it was simply the hand of God!

Allow me to share some eyewitness testimonies of the miracles in the Six-Day War.

THE CONQUEST OF SHECHEM

Israel's military commanders recognized that the taking of Shechem would be one of the toughest and bloodiest battles of the war. The largest crossing of the Jordan River began in the country of Jordan and continued through the Samarian Mountains and into the city of Shechem. Abraham used this very crossing as he entered into the land of Canaan (Genesis 12: 6).

The Jordanian army assumed that Israel would enter Shechem through their coastal region so they placed their heavy artillery and tanks on the other side of the city overlooking the roads leading to Shechem from the west. The IDF (Israel Defense Force) decided to outmaneuver the enemy by first fighting to the north and west and then coming back down to enter Shechem from the east, which was "the back door" of the city.

Colonel Uri Banari gives his eyewitness account:[8]

At the entrance to Shechem stood thousands of Arabs who waved white handkerchiefs and clapped their hands. In our naiveté, we returned greetings and smiles. We entered the town and wondered: We are advancing and there is no disorder, no panic, the local armed guards stand by with rifles in their hands keeping order, and the crowds are cheering.

Suddenly something happened which changed the entire picture in a moment. One of our officers wanted to disarm an Arab guard. When the latter refused, our officer fired a shot in the air. At that moment, all the crowds disappeared and streets emptied out. The Arabs began sniper fire.

I didn't comprehend what had transpired. Only later, did I understand.

The residents of Shechem thought that we were the Iraqi forces who were due to arrive from the direction of Jordan. The numerous enemy tanks were situated on the west side of Shechem. They woke up to their error very late.

The Arabs were surprised; the fear of the Jews fell upon them. In Hebron, and in Shechem, in Jenin and in Jericho the Arabs were heavily armed. There was not even one small Arab village without arms. With great haste, the Arabs, however, hid their weapons and didn't consider using them. They raised their hands up, and flew white flags of surrender from every edifice.

The fear of G-d fell upon hundreds of thousands of proud Arabs, who were filled with hatred and loathing for Israel. Only yesterday, they had sworn to fight until their last drop of blood.

A Direct Hit

In the late hours of the night, an IDF truck loaded with arms and shells parked next to a building in Jerusalem. Its mission was to bring a fresh supply of ammunition to the front line outposts. The element of danger was great for if the truck was hit by enemy fire, the subsequent explosions of all the ammo would bring all the buildings in the area down on their inhabitants.

Suddenly the whistling of an approaching enemy shell was

heard, and the shell, indeed, scored a direct hit on the vehicle. But the Arab shell did not explode. It remained perched atop the pile of Israeli shells in the truck.

Eighteen Against Two

Yisrael, a cab driver who was drafted to fight in the Six-Day War as part of the paratroop unit assigned with conquering the Straits of Tiran, gave the following account upon his return:

> The Israeli soldiers didn't have to parachute out of the Nord airplanes which took them to the Tiran Straits. They landed like spoiled tourists in the airport, because the Egyptian regiment which was on guard there fled before the Israeli troops were visible on the horizon.
>
> After landing, I was sent with another reserve soldier, an electrician, to patrol the area. When we had distanced ourselves two kilometers, an Egyptian halftrack appeared before us filled with soldiers and mounted with machine guns on every side. We had only light weapons with a few bullets that couldn't stop the halftrack for a second. We couldn't turn back, so we stood there in despair, waited for the first shot, and for lack of a better idea, aimed our guns at them.
>
> But the shots didn't come.
>
> The halftrack came to a halt, and we decided to

cautiously approach it. We found eighteen armed soldiers inside sitting with guns in hand, with a petrified look on their faces. They looked at us with great fear as though begging for mercy. I shouted "Hands up!"

As we were marching them and I had returned to a state of calm, I asked the Egyptian sergeant next to me, "Tell me, why didn't you shoot at us?"

He answered, "I don't know. My arms froze—they became paralyzed. My whole body was paralyzed, and I don't know why."

It turned out that these soldiers didn't know that the Straits of Tiran were already in Israeli hands; why didn't they eliminate us?

I don't have an answer. How can one say that G-d didn't help us.

THE FINGER OF GOD

IDF Director of Operations Maj. Gen. Ezer Weizmann was asked by Mr. Levanon, the father of a fallen pilot, how he explains the fact that for three straight hours, Israeli Air Force planes flew from one Egyptian airstrip to another destroying the enemy planes, yet the Egyptians did not radio ahead to inform their own forces of the oncoming Israeli attack.

Ezer Weizmann, who later served as president of the State of Israel, was silent. He then lifted his head and exclaimed, "The finger of G-d."

HA'ARETZ NEWSPAPER'S BOTTOM LINE

Following his blow-by-blow analysis, the military correspondent for the secular *Ha'aretz* newspaper summed up the Six-Day War with the admission: "Even a non-religious person must admit this war was fought with help from heaven."

A JOURNALIST'S EYEWITNESS ACCOUNT

A German journalist summarized:

> Nothing like this has happened in history. A force including 1,000 tanks, hundreds of artillery cannons, many rockets and fighter jets, and a hundred thousand soldiers armed from head to toe was destroyed in two days in an area covering hundreds of kilometers filled with reinforced outposts and installations.
>
> And this victory was carried out by a force that lost many soldiers and much equipment, positions, and vehicles. No military logic or natural cause can explain this monumental occurrence.

Scripture declares in Proverbs 21:1, "The king's heart is like channels of water in the hand of the LORD; He turns it wherever He wishes"(NASB).

King Hussein of Jordan proposed a cease-fire before the IDF could take back the Old City of Jerusalem. World leaders put increasing political pressure on Israel, demanding that they accept the proposed truce. Then suddenly, King Hussein changed his mind, refusing to submit to the very conditions of the cease-fire that he personally put in place! God's intervention allowed the IDF to bring the Old City under Israeli control.

The Old City had been under Jordanian control since 1948. For nineteen years the Jewish people had been prohibited from the Western Wall where they had prayed for thousands of years before. It took just three days for Israeli forces to defeat the Jordanian army. On the morning of June 7, the order was given to take back the Old City of Jerusalem.

Israeli paratroopers stormed the city and secured it. Defense Minister Moshe Dayan arrived with Chief of Staff Yitzhak Rabin to formally mark the Jews' return to their historic capital and their holiest site. At the Western Wall, the IDF's chaplain, Rabbi Shlomo Goren, blew a shofar to celebrate the event.

In total, 21,000 of Israel's enemies were killed during the Six-Day War; Israel lost 779 soldiers. Jerusalem became the capital of the Jewish people once again. David Ben-Gurion was right when he declared, "In Israel, in order to be a realist you must believe in miracles."

God's signature was on the miraculous victory of the Six-Day War. He signaled this historic event with the third series of Four Blood Moons. The trials and tribulation of war finally brought forth triumph for the Jewish people—the unification of their beloved Jerusalem.

> Oh, that salvation for Israel would come out of Zion!
> When the LORD restores his people, let Jacob rejoice
> and Israel be glad!
>
> (PSALM 14:7 NIV)

There will be a fourth series of Four Blood Moons in the near future. NASA has stated that this will be the last appearance of a Tetrad in this century. What historical event will take place during their occurrences that is significant to Israel and the Jewish people?

More importantly, what is God saying to mankind?

CHAPTER 16

The Four Blood Moons of 2014–15

Now when these things begin to happen,
look up and lift up your heads,
because your redemption draws near.

—LUKE 21:28

The next time the Four Blood Moons begin to appear will be in April of 2014. NASA has projected that the Tetrad will begin on April 2014 and end in September 2015.[1] It will occur in the following sequence:

1. Passover, April 15, 2014
2. Feast of Tabernacles, October 8, 2014
3. Passover, April 4, 2015
4. Feast of Tabernacles, September 28, 2015

BLOOD MOONS OF 2014–15

Passover April 15, 2014	Feast of Tabernacles October 8, 2014	**Total Solar Eclipse March 20, 2015**	Passover April 4, 2015	Feast of Tabernacles September 28, 2015

After the appearance of the second Blood Moon and before the third Blood Moon there will be a total solar eclipse on March 20, 2015.

What is the prophetic significance of these Four Blood Moons?

To help answer this very important question, we must review the journey we have taken since the beginning of this book.

It is very rare that Scripture, science, and historical events align with one another, yet the last three Four Blood Moon series or Tetrads have done exactly that. Remember, several Tetrads have occurred in the past five hundred years; only three have corresponded to the Jewish Feasts as well as being linked to historical events significant to Israel. Seven more Tetrads will take place in the twenty-first century, however only *one* of these seven, *the Tetrad of 2014–15,* will align itself with the Feasts of the Lord.

What were the common denominators of 1492, 1949, and 1967? They all centered on significant events related to Israel and the Jewish people, and they occurred on the Feasts of the Lord, but what about the future?

The Jewish people are *still* the apple of God's eye. They are *still* cherished and chosen of God. And they are *still* the people of covenant—a covenant God has pledged to keep forever. Therefore we can rightly conclude that the next series of Four Blood Moons of 2014 and 2015 will also hold significance for Israel and the Jewish people.

Each of the three previous series of Four Blood Moons began with a trail of tears and ended with triumph for the Jewish people.

The Old Testament prophets clearly state that when the Jewish people return from their second exile, they will never be removed from their covenant homeland again. Therefore, China, Iran, Russia, and the uprising of the Arab Spring will NOT remove the people from the land or the land of Israel from the earth!

God Almighty is going to defend Israel Himself, and Israel will prevail over all adversity and adversaries!

As we learned in chapter 1, the prophet Joel sends a clear and powerful message to the world and to Israel:

I will show wonders in the heavens and in the earth:

Blood and fire and pillars of smoke.

The sun shall be turned into darkness,

And the moon into blood,

Before the coming of the great and awesome day of the LORD.

(2:30–31)

The apostle Peter repeats Joel's declaration during his sermon on the day of Pentecost in the book of Acts (2:19–20). The prophet Joel and the apostle Peter are giving exactly the same message. Luke alerts us that when we see these signs (Luke 21:25), "Lift up your heads, because your redemption draws near" (Luke 21:28).

As mentioned earlier, I believe that the heavens are God's high-definition billboard. I believe that He has been sending signals and speaking to planet earth in the heavens since creation—we just haven't considered the meaning of the signals.

It bears repeating that King David acknowledged the heavens were God's billboard when he wrote:

The heavens declare the glory of God;

And the firmament shows His handiwork.

Day unto day utters speech,

And night unto night reveals knowledge.

There is no speech nor language

Where their voice is not heard.

Their line has gone out through all the earth,
And their words to the end of the world.

(PSALM 19:1–4)

PROPHETIC BULLS-EYE

Learning how to shoot a rifle in Texas is a rite of passage. My father gave me my first rifle when I was six years of age. It was a Marlin .22 caliber, and I carried it like Wyatt Earp going to the gun fight at the O.K. Corral.

It was a common practice for my older brother, Bill, and me to turn the hounds loose and to walk into the thick and tall Texas pine trees on hunting adventures that would make Tom Sawyer's exploits pale by comparison.

About the age of thirteen I was invited to go deer hunting for the first time with a member of our church. I checked in my .22 caliber rifle for a 30.06 with a four-power scope ready for the shot of the century.

Dad took me to the firing range to introduce me to the difference between the modest *pop* of my .22 and the *kaboom* of the 30.06. The first time I shot it I thought a mule had kicked me in the right shoulder.

Most importantly, I learned how to focus the scope on the 30.06. After several shots had numbed my right shoulder and had my ears ringing like church bells on New Year's Day, I could clearly see the target one hundred yards away.

Dad shouted, "Put the crosshairs of the scope on the

bull's-eye, then slowly squeeze the trigger—don't jerk it! Unless you hit the bull's-eye, all of your efforts are in vain."

When you focus on the coming Four Blood Moons by remembering the events that took place on the dates of past occurrences, when you set your sites on the signs of the terminal generation and concentrate on the concept of the Shemittah year, then you will clearly see your target, squeeze the trigger, and hit the bull's-eye! Remember the words of Jesus to His disciples on the Mount of Olives:

> So you also, when you see all these things, know that
> it [My coming] is near—at the doors! Assuredly, I say
> to you, this generation will by no means pass away till
> all these things take place.
>
> (MATTHEW 24:33–34)

Look at the word *generation*. When God was speaking to Abraham in Genesis 15, He labeled a generation as one hundred years. Some interpret the word *generation* in this passage as "race," meaning the Jewish people.

Jesus was presenting His Prophetic Conference to His twelve disciples, who were expecting the literal kingdom of God on earth in their lifetime.

Jesus was telling them that after the deception . . . after the wars and rumors of war . . . after the famines, the pestilence, and earthquakes in various places . . . after you are hated by all nations for My name's sake . . . after lawlessness, anarchy, and false prophets . . . after an abomination of desolation on the Temple Mount . . . after being scattered among the nations (AD 70) . . . and after Israel is reborn (May 1948)—*that* generation will see My return in the clouds of heaven. We *are* that generation!

SIGNS OF THE TERMINAL GENERATION

I have listed the signs of the terminal generation in several of my books[2] and some of them bear repeating, for we can't deny their existence and their importance to the next series of Blood Moons.

1. Rebirth of Israel
2. The Ingathering
3. Jewish control of Jerusalem
4. Deception on a global scale
5. The resurrection of the Hebrew language
6. The knowledge explosion
7. The birth of nuclear warfare

I have touched on the first four signs of the terminal generation in previous chapters; allow me to expound on the remaining three.

THE RESURRECTION OF THE HEBREW LANGUAGE

For then I will restore to the peoples a pure language,
That they all may call on the name of the LORD,
To serve Him with one accord.

(ZEPHANIAH 3:9)

The fulfillment of this prophecy began in 1881 when Eliezer Ben-Yehuda arrived in Palestine. Hebrew had not been the spoken language of the Jewish people since the time of the Bible and for centuries had been used only in study. Ben-Yehuda believed that Jewish nationalism was a twofold goal requiring the return of the Jewish people to their biblical homeland and the revival of the spoken Hebrew language.

Ben-Yehuda accomplished the nearly impossible feat of making Hebrew the modern language of the Jewish people yet never saw the creation of the State of Israel. He passed away only one month after British authorities declared Hebrew to be the official language of the Jews. His dream of the rebirth of the nation of Israel in its own land, speaking its own language, was a fulfillment of Bible prophecy.[3]

THE KNOWLEDGE EXPLOSION

But as for you, Daniel, conceal these words and seal up
the book until the end of time; many will go back and

forth, and knowledge will increase.

(DANIEL 12:4 NASB)

My parents were born at a time when the majority of people still traveled by horse-drawn carriages just as King David. In fact, not much had changed in the way of technology since the time of my great-grandparents. There were no telephones, no television, no faxes, no Xerox machines, and no computers! People communicated in person by letter, and only when someone died would you receive a telegram.

However, times have changed! Within the last few decades technology has exploded to the point that one can use a mobile phone to speak to anyone in the world and send messages via email, text, Twitter, and Facebook. We log on to the information highway by means of the Internet allowing access to any search engine available. You can watch your favorite television programs and movies through devices that can fit in your coat pocket. We share pictures, videos, and news *instantly*! Daily, this technology exponentially increases—just think of the number of times that you purchased the latest gizmo and it became obsolete before you walked out of the store!

There is no doubt that we are the generation that has experienced the knowledge explosion, but does more knowledge produce wisdom?

The fear of the LORD is the beginning of wisdom,

And the knowledge of the Holy One is understanding.

(PROVERBS 9:10)

THE BIRTH OF NUCLEAR WARFARE

This is the plague with which the LORD will strike all the nations that fought against Jerusalem: Their flesh will rot while they are still standing on their feet, their eyes will rot in their sockets, and their tongues will rot in their mouths. On that day people will be stricken by the LORD with great panic. They will seize each other by the hand and attack one another.

(ZECHARIAH 14:12–13 NIV)

Zechariah is describing the effects of an intense heat from a nuclear blast. What advances has man made in warfare technology since the time of this prophecy?

For eleven centuries, from AD 9 during the Tang Dynasty through the twentieth century, prior to WWII, the main source of warfare, using explosives, was gunpowder. Then in 1939 the Manhattan Project was born, ushering in the nuclear age with the invention of the atomic bomb, followed by the hydrogen bomb, which can produce 1.5 million degrees of heat in a fraction of second. This is why the Bible describes flesh falling from the body before the corpse can hit the ground.

The world still remembers the devastation of Hiroshima and Nagasaki, which were the only events in history where nuclear bombs were used in warfare. In the book of Revelation, John tells that four angels are going to be released to destroy one-third of the earth's population in one day. Before hydrogen bombs this was not possible! Now the world has enough nuclear power owned by the nations of the world to kill everyone on planet earth twenty times over.

Iran, with its radical religious leadership, has promised to share nuclear weapons with terrorist organizations around the globe. If and when Iran becomes nuclear, it will threaten and destabilize Western civilization. Iran's radical theology worships death, and a nuclear bomb will serve their theological concepts perfectly. It's only a matter of time before the nuclear genie is out of the bottle and a mushroom cloud covers the earth.

THE COMING SHEMITTAH YEAR

We detailed the importance of the Shemittah year in chapter 3. In short review, a Shemittah year occurs every seven years; it's known as a time of rest for the land much like the Sabbath, which occurs every seven days, is a time of rest for man. While *observing* Shemittah guarantees abundance, *neglecting* it leads to judgment.

Every seven years we experience a Shemittah year in which God allows something to happen that gets our undivided attention *whether we are ready or not!* Just look at what happened in the last several Shemittah years:

- The Shemittah year of 1973: The Supreme Court decision of Roe v. Wade occurred, which has resulted in the deaths of more 60 million unborn babies.
- The Shemittah year of 1980: Saddam Hussein invaded Iran to signal the beginning of the Gulf War years.
- The Shemittah year of 1987: A supernova that could be seen by the naked eye for the first time since 1604 occurred. A supernova is the explosion of a star that has reached the end of its life; this brilliant point of light can briefly outshine entire galaxies and radiate more energy than our sun will in its entire lifetime.[4] That same year the U.S. stock market crashed.
- The Shemittah year of 1994: Yasser Arafat returns to the Middle East. A rare earthquake occurred in North America on the New Madrid fault line; it spanned the Midwest of the United States up to Canada.
- The Shemittah year of 2001: America was attacked by radical Islamic terrorists killing nearly three thousand Americans on 9/11. This day became America's new day of infamy.
- The Shemittah year of 2008: America experienced a stock market crash on September 29 when the market fell 777 points in one day. It was the greatest one-day decline in the history of Wall Street.

Add seven years to 2008, and you have the year 2015, in which you also find the last two Four Blood Moons of 2014–15. Remember, God does everything at a "set time" (Psalm 102:13).

We know that only three Tetrads have occurred in the last 500 years that are significant to Israel and also fall on the Jewish Feasts. We also know that these are the only Tetrads that have had a total solar eclipse somewhere within the series. The coming Tetrad in 2014–15 will also contain a total solar eclipse within its series. But what is different between the previous three Tetrads significant to Israel and the coming Tetrad?

Unlike the others, this series of Four Blood Moons contains a Shemittah year beginning September 25, 2014, and concluding on September 13, 2015. Astoundingly, this Shemittah year will begin on the first day of the Jewish New Year (Feast of Trumpets) of 2014 and conclude on the following celebration of the Jewish New Year (Feast of Trumpets) in 2015. Follow this phenomenon:

- The occurrence of a lunar eclipse is common.
- The occurrence of a total lunar eclipse is less common.
- The occurrence of a Tetrad or four consecutive Blood Moons (total lunar eclipses) is rare.
- The occurrence of a Tetrad with a total solar eclipse within its series is very rare.
- A Tetrad with a total solar eclipse that is significant to

Israel's history and the Jewish Feasts is very, very rare.

- The occurrence of a Tetrad with a total solar eclipse historically significant to Israel and Jewish Feasts that includes a Shemittah year within its series is very, very, *very* rare.

- *But* a Tetrad with a total solar eclipse, historically significant to Israel and falling on the Jewish Feasts with a Shemittah year that corresponds with the Feast of Trumpets (the Jewish New Year) within its series is *astronomically rare!*

THE FEAST OF TRUMPETS

Say to the Israelites: "On the first day of the seventh month you are to have a day of sabbath rest, a sacred assembly commemorated with trumpet blasts. Do no regular work, but present a food offering to the LORD."

(LEVITICUS 23:24–25 NIV)

Shemittah Year

| Passover 4 / 15 / 14 | Rosh Hashanah Feast of Trumpets 9 / 25 / 14 | Feast of Tabernacles 10 / 8 / 14 | **Total Solar Eclipse 3 / 20 / 15** | Passover 4 / 4 / 15 | Rosh Hashanah Feast of Trumpets 9 / 13 / 15 | Feast of Tabernacles 9 / 28 / 15 |

Rosh Hashanah occurs on the first and second days of Tishri. In Hebrew, *Rosh Hashanah* means "head of the year" or "first of the year." Rosh Hashanah is commonly known as the Jewish New Year and is a time of introspection.

The name *Rosh Hashanah* is not used in the Bible. This holiday is instead referred to in the Hebrew as a day of remembrance or the day of the sounding of the shofar. It is called the Feast of Trumpets. One of the most important observances of this holiday is hearing the sound of the shofar (a ram's horn that sounds like a trumpet) in the synagogue. Some believe that the blowing of the trumpet is the call to repentance. Religious services for the holiday focus on the concept of God's sovereignty.

Another practice of the holiday is Tashlikh ("casting off"). Some of those observing this feast will walk through flowing water, such as a creek or river, on the afternoon of the first day and empty their pockets into the river, symbolically casting off their sins. The Shemittah year and Feast of Tabernacles begin at sunset September 25, 2014.

These occurrences are not coincidental! This is the hand of God orchestrating the signs in the heavens. The final Four Blood Moons are signaling that something big is coming . . . something that will change the world forever. But the bigger question is, are we watching and listening?

THE LIGHT OF ISRAEL

There have been sages within the centuries that have devoted their lives to the study of the Holy Scriptures. They have faithfully watched and waited for the signs in the heavens that God has given mankind. Now let's consider the foresights of one of these pious men, Rabbi Judah ben Samuel.

Rabbi Judah ben Samuel (1140–1217) was a legendary German rabbi of the twelfth century. He was an extremely devout man of God who gave a series of prophecies concerning the future of Jerusalem, all of which came true to the day.

Rabbi Samuel based his prophecies on the year of Jubilee. According to Leviticus 25, one Jubilee period is fifty years, in which during the fiftieth year each person would regain ownership of his or her land. All indentured servants were set free and all debts were forgiven.

The Ottoman Empire (Turks) captured the city of Jerusalem in 1517. Rabbi Samuel prophesied three hundred years previously that the Turks would control Jerusalem for eight Jubilees. Eight Jubilees would be eight times fifty—exactly four hundred years. The rabbi's prophecy came true! The Turks were conquered in 1917 when the British army, under the command of General Edmund Allenby, liberated Jerusalem on Hanukkah (the Festival of Lights), December 17, 1917.[5]

Rabbi Samuel's next prophecy stated, "Afterwards Jerusalem will become a no-man's land for one Jubilee."[6] Again, one Jubilee is fifty years.

What is the meaning of "no-man's land"? Exactly this: under the British Mandate the Jews were permitted to immigrate to what was then called Palestine, which is today Israel. While a limited number of Jews were permitted to immigrate into the land, they were not permitted to rule themselves; instead they were ruled by the British, who were favorable to the Arabs at the time.

As Rabbi Samuel had prophesied hundreds of years earlier, Palestine was indeed a "no-man's land"! The "no-man's land" prophecy was to end after one Jubilee, which was fifty years added to 1917—making it 1967, the year Jerusalem was reunited with the State of Israel and the Jewish people for the first time in nearly nineteen hundred years.

Rabbi ben Samuel's biblical calculations (Gematria) were purely theoretical; there was absolutely no sign at the time they were given of their fulfillment, for it was three hundred years after his death that the first prophecy would come to pass.

But independent of his yet-to-be-fulfilled foresights, Rabbi Judah ben Samuel's students testified that he was a godly man, a model of abstinence and selflessness who was waiting with a burning desire for the coming of the Messiah. The Rabbi was often called the "Light of Israel."

If anyone asked him where his wisdom came from he would answer, "The prophet Elijah, who will precede the Messiah, appeared to me and revealed many things to me and emphasized that the pre-condition to answered prayer is that it is fueled by enthusiasm and joy for the greatness and holiness of God."[7]

THE ISLAND OF FREEDOM

One of Israel's greatest prime ministers, Golda Meir once said, "Peace will come when the Arabs love their children more than they hate us." Since the nation of Israel became a state in 1948, they have endured repeated attacks and wars. They have constantly faced the threat of a hostile Arab world that wants to destroy them.

This nation that could fit inside the borders of Lake Michigan with room to spare is surrounded and greatly outnumbered by its enemies. Israel's survival from its inception to the present is surely a result of the Hand of God and the staggering sacrifice on the part of generation after generation of the Jewish people.

This island of democracy in the sea of an Arab-Islamic world sits at the center of constant religious and civil unrest. Just who are Israel's modern-day enemies and what is their current agenda?

ISRAEL'S HOSTILE NEIGHBORS

Israel's enemies can be divided into two groups: the surrounding Islamic nations that have historically been their opponents in past wars, and radical terrorist organizations formed more recently that are committed to Israel's destruction.

EGYPT

Egypt was the leading nation that fought against Israel in all of her past wars (1948, 1967, and 1973). Outlawed in Egypt since 1954, the Muslim Brotherhood emerged as a political party under a new name—the Freedom and Justice Party. Mohamed Morsi was a leading member of the Muslim Brotherhood and chairman of the Freedom and Justice Party. Morsi was voted in as the president of Egypt on June 30, 2012. The following is a quote from the former president:

> Either [you accept] the Zionists and everything they want, or else it is war. This is what these occupiers of the land of Palestine know—these blood-suckers, who attack the Palestinians, these warmongers, the descendants of apes and pigs.[8]

As *Four Blood Moons* goes to press, President Morsi has been ousted from office and placed under house arrest as a result of a "complete military coup" after thousands of Egyptian citizens demonstrated in the streets of Cairo demanding his resignation.

As of July 9, 2013, former Finance Minister Hazem el-Beblawi has been appointed Egypt's new prime minister. Only time will tell if the Muslim Brotherhood will allow the new regime to stay in power.[9]

SYRIA

Syria has been another opponent of Israel in all her past wars and remains an enemy of Israel to this day. Head of Hezbollah Political Council His Eminence Ibrahim Amin Sayyed laid out "dangers" facing the region, the first being the existence of Israel.

JORDAN

Jordan shares the longest border with Israel with a significantly large Sunni Muslim population. Although Jordan signed a peace treaty with Israel in 1994, the country is constantly under fire from Syria, which backs anti-Israel militants.[10]

IRAN

Iran is the greatest threat Israel currently faces. Under their fanatical former president, Mahmoud Ahmadinejad, Iran has been on a fast track to produce nuclear capabilities while promising to "wipe Israel off the map." Iran finances and trains Hamas and Hezbollah terrorists, equipping them with arms to use against Israel.

Consider this quote from the 2005 conference entitled "A World without Zionism" in Tehran, Iran:

> Our dear Imam said that the occupying regime must be
> wiped off the map and this was a very wise statement.
> We cannot compromise over the issue of Palestine. Is

it possible to create a new front in the heart of an old front. This would be a defeat and whoever accepts the legitimacy of this regime [Israel] has in fact, signed the defeat of the Islamic world. Our dear Imam targeted the heart of the world oppressor in his struggle, meaning the occupying regime (Israel). I have no doubt that the new wave that has started in Palestine, and we witness it in the Islamic world too, will eliminate this disgraceful stain from the Islamic world. But we must be aware of tricks.[11]

A TARGET FOR TERRORISTS

While the nations of the Middle East present the visible threat to Israel's existence, radical Islamic organizations such as the PLO, Hamas, Hezbollah, and Fatah are an ever-present force inciting strife and bloodshed, and providing momentum for an increasingly hostile and unstable environment for Israel. Fueled by perceived success in their last armed conflict with Israel, they are committed to an all-out war with Israel in the near future.

It is 1967 all over again.

The coming Four Blood Moons are aligning themselves, the next Shemittah year is nearing, the sages of old have foretold of events past and those to come, the enemies of Israel are surrounding the Land of Covenant once again, the signs of the terminal generation are complete . . . there is only one question left to answer. . . .

Are You Ready?

The fourth series of Four Blood Moons is coming! They are extremely rare even by scientific standards. God is shouting to us, "Something big is about to happen!" However, the coming Four Blood Moons of 2014–15 does not mean the Rapture is going to happen during that time. Why? Because the Rapture could happen at any moment.

What they *are* telling us is that God is getting ready to change the course of human history once again. He is preparing to display the next series of signs in the heavens. What is going to happen?

The question is not about the terminal generation or when Israel's enemies are going to attack next—the question is are *you* ready to meet the Lord? Are *your* children ready?

Watch and pray! Be prepared, like the five wise virgins who made sure they had extra oil for their lamps (Matthew 25:13). The Church is soon to leave the world. We are seeing signs of the end of this age.

Jesus said, "When these signs begin to happen, look up and lift up your heads, because your redemption draws near" (Luke 21:28).

We're getting ready to leave here. The King is coming! He is coming soon with power and great glory, and His reward is with Him (Isaiah 40:10). Are you ready? Are the members of your family ready? It's the greatest question you will ever answer in this life!

When you see these signs in the heavens, don't be afraid; rather lift up your heads and rejoice. Shout for joy! Your redemption draws nigh. The battle is over; soon we shall wear a robe and a crown of life.

> There will be signs in the sun, in the moon, and in the stars; and on the earth distress of nations, with perplexity, the sea and the waves roaring; *men's hearts failing them from fear and the expectation of those things which are coming on the earth*, for the powers of the heavens will be shaken. Then they will see the Son of Man coming in a cloud with power and great glory. *Now when these things begin to happen, look up and lift up your heads, because your redemption draws near.*
>
> (LUKE 21:25–28)

Charles Haddon Spurgeon, the great English preacher of the nineteenth century, didn't speak extensively concerning the end times. But what he did say showed a remarkable understanding concerning the interrelationship of the things to come and the return of Christ as recorded in the book of Luke.

The following are excerpts from his sermon entitled "Joyful Anticipation of the Second Advent":

> I must leave this first point, concerning the terrible time (a time of fearful national trouble) when this

precept is to be carried out, by just reminding you that, when the Lord Jesus Christ shall come, the heavens shall tell us: "There shall be signs in the sun, and in the moon, and in the stars." Now I come to THE REMARKABLE PRECEPT itself: "Then I look up; lift up your heads."

Let there be no looking down because the earth is quaking and shaking, but let there be a looking up because you are going to rise from it; no looking down because the graves are opening; why should you look down?

You will quit the grave, never more to die. "Lift up your heads." The time for you to hang your heads, like bulrushes, is over already, and will certainly be over when the Lord is coming, and your redemption draweth nigh. Wherefore, "look up, and lift up your heads." Hallelujah![12]

The coming Four Blood Moons are almost here ... are you ready?

NOTES

CHAPTER 1: SIGNS IN THE HEAVENS

1. "Russian meteor exploded with force of 30 Hiroshima bombs," *The Telegraph*, February 16, 2013, http://www.telegraph.co.uk/science/space/9874662/Russian-meteor-exploded-with-force-of-30-Hiroshima-bombs.html.

2. "Russian Meteor: Lack of Fragments Sparks Conspiracy Theories," *The Telegraph*, February 16, 2013, http://www.telegraph.co.uk/science/space/9874790/Russian-meteor-lack-of-fragments-sparks-conspiracy-theories.html.

3. Tariq Malik, "Giant Sun Eruption Captured in NASA Video," Space.com, November 17, 2012, http://www.space.com/18533-giant-sun-eruption-nasa-video.html.

4. Michio Kaku interview with George Norry, *Coast to Coast*, November 24, 2012, http://www.amateurastronomers.net/youtube-interviews.html.

5. Michio Kaku, "We Are Sitting Ducks for Solar Flares," Big Think, February 1, 2012, http://bigthink.com/videos/we-are-sitting-ducks-for-solar-flares.

CHAPTER 2: THE STAR IN THE EAST

1. John Phillips, *Exploring Genesis: An Expository Commentary* (Grand Rapids, MI: Kregel Publications, 2001), 38.

2. "How Hot Is the Sun?" Space.com, http://www.space.com/17137-how-hot-is-the-sun.html.

3. Andrew Grant, "100. Sun Burn," *Discover*, January-February 2013, 92, http://discovermagazine.com/2013/jan-feb/100-sun-burn#.UUMrUhysiSo.

CHAPTER 3: WARNING COMES BEFORE JUDGMENT

1. Space.com, http://www.space.com/15689-lunar-eclipses.html.

2. Space.com, http://www.space.com/15689-solar-eclipses.html.

3. Rabbi Moshe Pinchuk, Director of Jewish Heritage Center, Netanya Academic College, June 2013, http://www.staff.science.uu.nl/~gent0113/eclipse/eclipsecycles.htm.

4. http://www.timeanddate.com/calendar/roman-calendar.html/.

5. http://www.timeanddate.com/calendar/julian-calendar.html/.

6. http://www.timeanddate.com/calendar/gregorian-calendar.html/.

7. Clarence Larkin, *Dispensational Truth* (Glenside, PA: Rev. Clarence Larkin Est., 1920).

8. David Wessel, "Did the 'Great Depression' Live Up to the Name?" *Wall Street Journal*, April 8, 2010.

CHAPTER 4: THE SPINE OF PROPHECY

1. *The (Online) Book of Common Prayer*, "The Great Litany," http://www.bcponline.org/.

2. Flavius Josephus, *The Jewish War: Revised Edition* (New York: Penguin Classics, 1984), 1.

3. "*Tisha B'Av* [The 9th of Av]," Judaism 101, http://www.jewfaq.org/holidayd.htm.

CHAPTER 6: CONCERNING THE RAPTURE

1. Dietrich Bonhoeffer, cited in Eric Metaxas, *Bonhoeffer: Pastor, Martyr, Prophet, Spy* (Nashville: Thomas Nelson, 2010), back flap.

2. Arthur W. Pink, *Gleanings in Genesis* (Chicago: Moody, 1922), 5, http://books.google.com/books?id=He89UcODFyIC&pg=PA20&source=gbs_toc_r&cad=4#v=snippet&q=trinity&f=false.

3. Portions of this description can be found in John Hagee's *Can America Survive?*, updated edition (Nashville: Howard Books, 2011), 219.

4. J. Vernon McGee, *Thru the Bible* (Nashville: Thomas Nelson Publishers, 1983), vol. 4, p. 95 and vol. 5, p. 726–27.

5. McGee, *Thru the Bible*, vol. 3, p. 673.

CHAPTER 7: LAND OF PROMISE, LAND OF PAIN

1. Dan Senor and Saul Singe, *Startup Nation: The Story of Israel's Economic Miracles* (New York: Twelve/Hachette Book Group, 2009), 13–15.

2. Eric H. Cline, *From Eden to Exile: Unraveling Mysteries of the Bible* (Washington, DC: National Geographic Society, 2007), 43–53.

CHAPTER 8: WARS AND RUMORS OF WARS

1. "Origins of the Balfour Declaration," The Balfour Declaration, Zionism, November 2, 1917, http://www.zionism-israel.com/Balfour_Declaration_1917.htm.

2. "The Road to War: Germany: 1919–1939," AuthenticHistory.com, http://www.authentichistory.com/1930-1939/4-roadtowar/1-germany/.

3. *Daily Alert*, "Why You Shouldn't Get Too Excited about Rowhani" (June 21, 2013), http://www.dailyalert.org/rss/tagpage.php?id=45520.

4. Harry S Truman, "Why I Dropped the Bomb," cited in Margaret Truman, ed., *Where the Buck Stops: The Personal and Private Writings of Harry S Truman* (New York: Warner Books, 1989).

5. "Holocaust Evidence: Eisenhower's Proof," Awesome Stories, http://www.awesomestories.com/history/holocaust-evidence/eisenhowers-proof.

6. Stephen E. Atkins, *Holocaust Denial As an International Movement* (Westport, CT: Praeger Publishers, 2009), 216.

7. Paul Harvey, "If I Were the Devil" transcript: cited on Jackson Adams, "The Paul Harvey Excerpt That Didn't Make the Super Bowl," *The American Spectator*, February 4, 2013, http://spectator.org/blog/2013/02/04/the-paul-harvey-excerpt-that-w.

CHAPTER 9: FAMINE, EARTHQUAKES, AND ANARCHY

1. worldhunger.org.

2. arc.org.

3. "The Family Farm Is Being Systemically Wiped Out of Existence in America," The Economic Collapse, April 26, 2012, http://theeconomiccollapseblog.com/archives/the-family-farm-is-being-systematically-wiped-out-of-existence-in-america.

4. Ibid.

5. Department of Treasury, Federal Reserve Board, June 14, 2013.

6. Emily Miller, "Death Tax Hike to 55% Nears," Human Events, December 1, 2010, http://www.humanevents.com/2010/12/01/death-tax-hike-to-55-nears/.

7. Associated Press (February 15, 2013).

8. Examiner.com (January 11, 2013).

9. Otto W. Nuttli, *The Effects of Earthquakes in the Central United States* (Marble Hill, MO: Gutenberg-Richter Publications, 1993), 41–48.

10. "Wisconsin Battle over Union Rights Shifts to Recall Efforts, High Court Election," FoxNews.com, April 12, 2011, http://www.foxnews.com/politics/2011/04/12/wisconsin-battle-union-rights-shifts-recall-efforts-high-court-election/.

11. Michael S. Schmidt and Colin Moyhihan, "F.B.I. Counterrorism Agents Monitored Occupy Movement, Records Show," *New York Times*, December 24, 2012, http://www.nytimes.com/2012/12/25/nyregion/occupy-movement-was-investigated-by-fbi-counterterrorism-agents-records-show.html.

12. Ibid.

13. "Florida Student Claims He Was Suspended for Refusing to 'Stomp on Jesus' in Class," Fox News Insider, March 23, 2013, http://foxnewsinsider.com/2013/03/23/students-told-to-stomp-on-jesus-at-florida-atlantic-university-by-professor-deandre-poole/.

14. Gary L. Bauer, "Liberal Inanity," Campaign for Working Families, March 5, 2013, http://www.cwfpac.com/eod/tuesday-march-5-2013.

15. Ibid.

Chapter 10: The Gospel of the Kingdom

1. *Coliseum and Christian Martyrs Encyclopedia,* http://
www.tribunesandtriumphs.org/colosseum/colosseum-
christian-martyrs.htm.
2. "Aelia Capitolina: Judaism Expelled," GoJerusalem.
com, http://www.gojerusalem.com/article_520/
Aelia-Capitolina-Judaism-Expelled.
3. http://www.sacred-texts.com/jud/josephus/war-1.htm
(chapter 1, section 2).
4. Tsafrir Ronen, "Hadrian's Curse—The Invention
of Palestine," CrethiPlethi.com, May 22, 2010,
http://www.crethiplethi.com/hadrians-curse-the-
invention-of-palestine/israel/2010/.

Chapter 12: Four Blood Moons and Two Feasts

1. Bill Koenig, *World Watch Daily,* Koenig International
News, http://watch.org/showprint.php3?idx=
104119&mcat=24&rtn=index.html.
2. http://www.jewfaq.org/holiday5.htm.

Chapter 13: The Four Blood Moons of 1493–94

1. Mark Blitz, *The Feasts of the Lord*, El Shaddai Ministries
(Bonney Lake, WA 98391).

2. Henry Kamen, *Spanish Inquisition* (New Haven, CT: Yale University Press, 1999), 49.

3. H. H. Ben-Sasson, ed. *A History of the Jewish People* (Cambridge, MA: Harvard University Press, 1976), 588–590.

4   *Encyclopedia Judaica*; The Spanish Inquisition Gates to Jewish Heritage.

5. Barbara Epstein, *The Minsk Ghetto 1941–1943: Jewish Resistance and Soviet Internationalism* (Berkeley, CA: University of California Press, 2008).

6   *Encyclopedia Judaica*, vol. 15 (Jerusalem: Keter, 1972), 235.

7. Ibid.

8. Joseph Telushkin, *Jewish Literacy: The Most Important Things to Know About the Jewish Religion, Its People, and Its History* (New York: William Morrow, 1991).

9. 2000–2011 Jewish-American Hall of Fame © 2012 American Numismatic Society.

10. Dagobert D. Runes, *The War Against the Jew* (New York: Philosophical Library, 2008), 171.

11. Ibid., 12.

12. Ibid., 12–13.

13. Ibid., 160.

14. Elinor and Robert Slater, *Great Moments in Jewish History* (Jerusalem: Jonathan David Publishers, 1998), 170.

15. Ibid., 170–71.

16. Hakevi, "Al-queda: The Next Goal Is to Liberate Spain from the Infidels," Jerusalem Center for Public Affairs, Vol 7, no. 16, Oct 11, 2007.

CHAPTER 14: THE FOUR BLOOD MOONS OF 1949–50

1. NASA Eclipse Web site, http://eclipse.gsfc.nasa.gov/eclipse.html.
2. The Jewish Virtual Library, Establishment of Israel: The Declaration of the Establishment of the State of Israel, http://www.jewishvirtuallibrary.org/jsource/biography/Herzl.html.
3. Menachim Begin, *The Revolt: Story of the Irgun* (Jerusalem: Steimatzky Agency Ltd; 1977).
4. "The Bombing of the King David Hotel," Jewish Virtual Library, http://www.jewishvirtuallibrary.org/jsource/History/King_David.html.
5. "British White Paper of 1939," Jewish Virtual Library, http://www.jewishvirtuallibrary.org/jsource/History/paper39.html.
6. The Jewish Virtual Library, Establishment of Israel: The Declaration of the Establishment of the State of Israel.
7. http://www.britannica.com/EBchecked/topic/60297/David-Ben-Gurion.
8. The Jewish Virtual Library, Establishment of Israel: The Declaration of the Establishment of the State of Israel.

CHAPTER 15: THE FOUR BLOOD MOONS OF 1967–68

1. Isi Leibler, *The Case For Israel* (Australia: The Globe Press, 1972) 60.

2. Ibid.

3. Ibid.

4. Ibid., 18.

5. Ibid., 60.

6. Ibid., 18.

7. Chaim Herzog, *The Arab-Israeli Wars* (New York: Random House, 1982), 149.

8. Original text on pages 215–19 from R. Menachem Mendel Kasher, *The Great Era* (Torah Shelemah Institute).

CHAPTER 16: THE FOUR BLOOD MOONS OF 2014–15

1. http://eclispe.gsfc.nasa.gov/eclipse.html.

2. John Hagee, *The Battle for Jerusalem* (Nashville: Thomas Nelson Publishers, 2001), 103–117; John Hagee, *Jerusalem Countdown* (Lake Mary, FL: Frontline, 2007), 127; John Hagee, *Can America Survive* (Nashville: Howard Books), 189–211.

3. http://www.myjewishlearning.com/culture/2/Languages/Hebrew/History_and_Centrality/Eliezer_Ben_Yehuda.shtml?p=3.

4. http://www.space.com/6638-supernova.html.

5. "Timeline 1916–1917," Timelines of History, http://timelines.ws/20thcent/1916_1917.HTML.

6. Rabbi Judah ben Samuel, "Jubilee Prophecy Gives the Year of the Messiah," Destination Yisra'el, December 2, 2012, http://destination-yisrael.biblesearchers.com/destination-yisrael/2012/12/rabbi-judah-ben-samuels-jubilee-prophecy-gives-the-year-of-the-messiah.html.

7. Mark Blitz, *The Feasts of the Lord*.

8. The Commentator, http://www.thecommentator.com/article/2360/mohammed_morsi_on_israel_these_blood_suckers_these_warmongers_the_descendants_of_apes_and_pigs#.UdGPr-2nLFU.email.

9. Fox News (with the Associated Press and Reuters contributing to this report), http://www.foxnews.com/world/2013/07/05/egyptian-islamists-to-protest-morsi-removal-amid-reports-violence-arrests/.

10. http://www.ynetnews.com/articles/0,7340,L-4369856,00.html.

11. http://www.nytimes.com/2005/10/30weekinreview/30iran.html?pagewanted=all&_r=0.

12. Charles Hadden Spurgeon, Metropolitan Tabernacles Pulpit Vol. 42, (Pilgrim Publication, 1998), 2496.

About the Author

John Hagee is the author of several *New York Times* bestsellers, in addition to *Jerusalem Countdown*, which sold over one million copies. He is the founder and senior pastor of Cornerstone Church in San Antonio, Texas, a nondenominational evangelical church with more than twenty thousand active members, as well as the founder and president of John Hagee Ministries, which telecasts his radio and television teachings throughout America and in 249 nations worldwide. Hagee is also the founder and national chairman of Christians United for Israel, a national grassroots association with over one million members to date.

WORTHY
PUBLISHING

If you enjoyed this book, will you consider
sharing the message with others?

- Mention the book in a Facebook post, Twitter update,
  Pinterest pin, or blog post.

- Recommend this book to those in your small group,
  book club, workplace, and classes.

- Head over to www.facebook.com/JohnHageeMinistries,
  "LIKE" the page, and post a comment as to what you
  enjoyed the most.

- Tweet "I recommend reading #FourBloodMoons by
  @PastorJohnHagee // @worthypub" // #BloodMoons

- Pick up a copy for someone you know who would be
  challenged and encouraged by this message.

- Write a review on amazon.com, bn.com, goodreads.com,
  or cbd.com.

**You can subscribe to Worthy Publishing's newsletter at
www.worthypublishing.com**

**WORTHY PUBLISHING
FACEBOOK PAGE**

**WORTHY PUBLISHING
WEBSITE**